A MATTER
OF ETERNITY

A MATTER
OF ETERNITY

SELECTIONS FROM THE WRITINGS OF
DOROTHY L. SAYERS

CHOSEN AND INTRODUCED BY
ROSAMOND KENT SPRAGUE

WILLIAM B. EERDMANS PUBLISHING COMPANY
GRAND RAPIDS, MICHIGAN

Copyright © 1973 by William B. Eerdmans Publishing Company
All rights reserved
ISBN 0-264-64626-6
Printed in the United States of America
First published in Great Britain, 1973
by A. R. Mowbray & Co. Ltd.
The Alden Press, Osney Mead, Oxford

A MATTER OF ETERNITY
Copyright 1947, Dorothy L. Sayers

Contents

Acknowledgments

My special thanks are due to Miss Muriel St. Clare Byrne, O.B.E., for allowing me to include the previously unpublished poem "For Timothy, in the Coinherence." Permission to use the remaining selections was graciously given by Mr. Anthony Fleming and his English agent David Higham.

Almighty God, Father of Heaven, send down, we beseech Thee, Thy blessing upon this our undertaking. Blessed Lord Jesus Christ, Word of God, Son of the Father, assist us with Thy wisdom. Holy Spirit of God, be present with us and guide us into all truth. Amen.

EC 137-138

Abbreviations

BH	*Begin Here: A War-Time Essay.* London: Victor Gollancz, 1940.
CC	*Creed or Chaos.* New York: Harcourt Brace and Company, 1949.
Hell	Dante, *The Divine Comedy (Hell),* tr. Dorothy L. Sayers. Harmondsworth: Penguin Books, Limited, 1949.
Purg.	Dante, *The Divine Comedy (Purgatory),* tr. Dorothy L. Sayers. Harmondsworth: Penguin Books, Limited, 1955.
DTP	*The Devil to Pay: A Stage-Play.* New York: Harcourt Brace and Company, 1939.
EC	*The Emperor Constantine: A Chronicle.* London: Victor Gollancz, 1951.
FPD	*Further Papers on Dante.* New York: Harper and Brothers, 1957.
GDS	*The Greatest Drama Ever Staged.* London: Hodder and Stoughton, 1938 (pamphlet).
IPD	*Introductory Papers on Dante.* New York: Harper and Brothers, 1954.
LTL	*The Lost Tools of Learning.* London: Methuen, 1948 (pamphlet).
MBTK	*The Man Born to Be King: A Play Cycle on the Life of Our Lord and Saviour Jesus Christ.* London: Victor Gollancz, 1943.
MM	*The Mind of the Maker.* New York: Harcourt Brace and Company, 1941.

PSPS   *The Poetry of Search and the Poetry of State-ment.* London: Victor Gollancz, 1963.

UD   *Unnatural Death (The Dawson Pedigree).* New York: Harper and Brothers, 1955.

UO   *Unpopular Opinions: Twenty-One Essays.* New York: Harcourt Brace and Company, 1947.

WB   *Whose Body?* New York: Harper and Brothers, n.d.

ZH   *The Zeal of Thy House* (with a preface by Laurence Irving). London: Victor Gollancz, 1949.

Introduction

Perhaps most of the readers of this book who already know something of the work of Dorothy L. Sayers will come to it fresh, so to speak, from the arms of Peter Wimsey. Not a few will make this transition with surprise, and certainly there are some who will do so with resentment. I have known Sayers devotees to react with disgust and fury to the news that Wimsey's creator had turned to the writing of religious drama. As one who has made the transition in the reverse direction, from *The Man Born to Be King* to *Whose Body?* and *The Unpleasantness at the Bellona Club,* I would wish to maintain that Dorothy L. Sayers is a remarkably consistent writer who does not change her basic characteristics and concerns in spite of changing her subject-matter.

Consider, for instance, the end of *Busman's Honeymoon.* It is a very rare detective-writer who carries the reader to events beyond the identification of the murderer. Peter's visits to the prison in search of the condemned man's forgiveness (which he does not in fact receive) and his vigil before the execution are certainly best understood as evidences of a theological concern. Or consider specifically Christian characters such as Miss Kitty Climpson (in *Unnatural Death* and *Strong Poison*) and Mr. Venables (in *The Nine Tailors*). At first both appear to be stock figures: a mildly ludicrous elderly spinster and a bumbling absent-minded clergyman. But as we come to know them, certain rocklike qualities begin to emerge—and this rock is Christ.

Lord Peter, of course, is not a Christian and shows no signs of becoming one. For specific information on this point, the reader may like to consult the passages from *The Mind of the Maker* and *Unnatural Death* that are included in the section headed "Creation."

11

The remarkable consistency of Miss Sayers' writing again became evident when, after choosing the pieces for this book, I began to assign them to different categories. One of her major topics was clearly work, but passages on this subject tended to stray towards creation, or, if *bad* work were in question, towards sin. Dogma and drama were certainly hard to keep apart in one who had stated that "the dogma *is* the drama," and there was another thin dividing line between dogma, reality, and history. No doubt she would have been the first to say that the consistency was not hers but that of the faith that informed her thought.

Dorothy L. Sayers was a robust enemy of uninformed and slipshod thinking; it appalled her that the Christian faith should be rejected by persons who had never taken the trouble to find out what it was. Consequently I have included quite a number of passages that simply state what certain Christian doctrines *are*. The seven deadly sins are defined, and under "Purgatory" considerable information is given as to what this rather (to Anglicans) unfamiliar doctrine means. Nor was she one to obscure or omit the less palatable truths of the Gospel. She reminds us, for example, that "we cannot repudiate Hell without altogether repudiating Christ." But if this is bad news, she has given us abundant proclamation of the good news of the redeeming power of Our Lord:

> God did not abolish the fact of evil: He transformed it.
> He did not stop the crucifixion: He rose from the dead.

The religious plays, notably those of the marvellous radio series on the life of Christ entitled *The Man Born to Be King,* are badly under-represented in this book, owing to the difficulty of making neat incisions in continuous dialogue. These plays should not be missed, nor should the fascinating introductory material that tells of a craftsman's approach to the special technical problems of religious drama for radio. And, for a full-length demonstration of the fact that Christian doctrine is genuinely dramatic, try *The Emperor Constantine*. If you think the Council of Nicaea an unpromising topic for a play, prepare for a change of mind!

Except for the brief essay, *Christian Morality*, I have included only one complete piece of any length in this book, the pamphlet entitled *The Lost Tools of Learning*. Since the topic is education, the choice may seem an odd one for a devotional book. I would defend the choice, however, by pointing out that Miss Sayers regarded education as a matter for the whole man, as she regarded Christianity as a whole man's faith. This faith has, after all, a content to be assimilated, and this assimilation requires a properly instructed mind.

It may be asked whether the book has any especial relevance to the concerns of the 1970's beyond the timeless proclamation of Christian fact. Two topics come particularly to mind: women and humanism. Miss Sayers regarded women as human beings first and females second, a point salutary for some of us to remember at the present time. As to humanism, she is surely perceptively right when she finds its basic flaw to be the misunderstanding of evil. To regard human nature as totally rational is to be as baffled by deliberate malignity as, indeed, to be bewildered by the Divine charity.

I once had the privilege of hearing a lecture by Dorothy L. Sayers. At the Canterbury Festival of 1951 she spoke to a captivated audience on "Change-ringing." I remember two particular things about the content of the lecture. The first was that she informed us that she had got up the subject of campanology for the specific purpose of writing *The Nine Tailors* — thus providing an apt if unconscious illustration of what she has written in *The Lost Tools of Learning*:

> For the tools of learning are the same, in any and every subject; and the person who knows how to use them will, at any age, get the mastery of a new subject in half the time and with a quarter of the effort expended by the person who has not the tools at his command.

Secondly — and I am sure that no one there could possibly forget this — she divided us into three groups, each group to represent the note of a different bell, and set us to work to illustrate the lecture. Not only was this an excellent teaching device, but everyone enjoyed it — we were *creating* something. And to create is, in her view, a trinitarian and thus a specifically Christian function: this is the basic theme of *The Mind of the Maker,* the book that can be said to be the summation of her theological thinking.

We are fortunate that in our century a person of so much verve and creative power should have chosen to put her finely tempered mind at the service of her Savior and His Church.

ROSAMOND KENT SPRAGUE

The Man

*I*F CHRIST is not true God equally with the Father, there is no essential difference between Christianity and pagan polytheism.

EC 108

For Jesus Christ is unique—unique among gods and men. There have been incarnate gods a-plenty, and slain-and-resurrected gods not a few; but He is the only God who has a date in history. And plenty of founders of religions have had dates, and some of them have been prophets or avatars of the Divine; but only this one of them was personally God. There is no more astonishing collocation of phrases than that which, in the Nicene Creed, sets these two statements flatly side by side: "Very God of very God. . . . He suffered under Pontius Pilate." All over the world, thousands of times a day, Christians recite the name of a rather undistinguished Roman pro-consul —not in execration (Judas and Caiaphas, more guilty, get off with fewer reminders of their iniquities), but merely because that name fixes within a few years the date of the death of God.

MBTK 20-21

. . . if the Church is to make any impression on the modern mind we will have to preach Christ and the cross.

CC 36

The people who hanged Christ never, to do them justice, accused Him of being a bore—on the contrary; they thought Him too dynamic to be safe. It has been left for later generations to muffle up that shattering personality and surround Him with an atmosphere of tedium. We

have very efficiently pared the claws of the Lion of Judah,
certified Him "meek and mild," and recommended Him
as a fitting household pet for pale curates and pious old
ladies. To those who knew Him, however, He in no way
suggested a milk-and-water person; *they* objected to Him
as a dangerous firebrand. True, He was tender to the unfortunate, patient with honest inquirers, and humble before Heaven; but He insulted respectable clergymen by
calling them hypocrites; He referred to King Herod as
"that fox"; He went to parties in disreputable company
and was looked upon as a "gluttonous man and a winebibber, a friend of publicans and sinners"; He assaulted
indignant tradesmen and threw them and their belong-
ings out of the Temple; He drove a coach-and-horses
through a number of sacrosanct and hoary regulations;
He cured diseases by any means that came handy, with a
shocking casualness in the matter of other people's pigs
and property; He showed no proper deference for wealth
or social position; when confronted with neat dialectical
traps, He displayed a paradoxical humour that affronted
serious-minded people, and He retorted by asking dis-
agreeably searching questions that could not be answered
by rule of thumb. He was emphatically not a dull man in
His human lifetime, and if He was God, there can be
nothing dull about God either. But He had "a daily
beauty in His life that made us ugly," and officialdom
felt that the established order of things would be more
secure without Him. So they did away with God in the
name of peace and quietness.

CC 5-6

It seems that wherever there is a suffering God, there is
an end of tragic futility, and a transvaluation of all values. . . . The disciples of Jesus, plunged into cowardice
and despondency by the human tragedy of the Crucifix-

ion, needed only to be convinced by the Resurrection that that which had suffered and died was in actual historical fact the true Being of all things, to recover their courage and spirits in a manner quite unparalleled, and to proclaim the Divine Comedy loudly and cheerfully, with the utmost disregard for their own safety. Why and how the suffering of God should have this exhilarating effect upon the human spirit is a question for Atonement theology; that it had this effect on those who believed in it is plain.

MBTK 27-28

The Christian formula is not: "Humanity manifests certain adumbrations of the divine", but: "*This* man was very God." On that pivot of singularity the whole Christian interpretation of phenomena uncompromisingly turns.

Purg. 39

They mocked and railed on Him and smote Him, they scourged and crucified Him. Well, they were people very remote from ourselves, and no doubt it was all done in the noblest and most beautiful manner. We should not like to think otherwise.

Unhappily, if we think about it at all, we must think otherwise. God was executed by people painfully like us, in a society very similar to our own—in the over-ripeness of the most splendid and sophisticated Empire the world has ever seen. In a nation famous for its religious genius and under a government renowned for its efficiency, He was executed by a corrupt church, a timid politician, and a fickle proletariat led by professional agitators. His executioners made vulgar jokes about Him, called him filthy names, taunted Him, smacked Him in the face, flogged

Him with the cat, and hanged Him on the common
gibbet—a bloody, dusty, sweaty, and sordid business.

If you show people that, they are shocked. So they
should be. If that does not shock them, nothing can. If
the mere representation of it has an air of irreverence,
what is to be said about the deed? It is curious that people
who are filled with horrified indignation whenever a cat
kills a sparrow can hear that story of the killing of God
told Sunday after Sunday and not experience any shock
at all.

MBTK 22-23

If we did not know all His retorts by heart, if we had not
taken the sting out of them by incessant repetition in the
accents of the pulpit, and if we had not somehow got it
into our heads that brains were rather reprehensible, we
should reckon Him among the greatest wits of all time.
Nobody else, in three brief years, has achieved such an
output of epigram.

MBTK 26

"The Kingdom of Heaven", said the Lord Christ, "is
among you." But what, precisely, is the Kingdom of
Heaven? You cannot point to existing specimens, saying,
"Lo, here!" or "Lo, there!" You can only experience it.
But what is it like, so that when we experience it we may
recognize it? Well, it is a change, like being born again
and re-learning everything from the start It is secret,
living power—like yeast. It is something that grows, like
seed. It is precious like buried treasure, like rich pearl,
and you have to pay for it. It is a sharp cleavage through
the rich jumble of things which life presents: like fish
and rubbish in a draw-net, like wheat and tares; like wisdom and folly; and it carries with it a kind of menacing

finality; it is new, yet in a sense it was always there—like turning out a cupboard and finding there your own childhood as well as your present self; it makes demands, it is like an invitation to a royal banquet—gratifying, but not to be disregarded, and you have to live up to it; where it is equal, it seems unjust, where it is just it is clearly not equal—as with the single pound, the diverse talents, the labourers in the vineyard, you have what you bargained for; it knows no compromise between an uncalculating mercy and a terrible justice—like the unmerciful servant, you get what you give; it is helpless in your hands like the King's Son, but if you slay it, it will judge you; it was from the foundations of the world; it is to come; it is here and now; it is within you. It is recorded that the multitude sometimes failed to understand.

PSPS 281

Not Herod, not Caiaphas, not Pilate, not Judas ever contrived to fasten upon Jesus Christ the reproach of insipidity; that final indignity was left for pious hands to inflict. To make of His story something that could neither startle, nor shock, nor terrify, nor excite, nor inspire a living soul is to crucify the Son of God afresh and put Him to an open shame.

MBTK 37

The Dogma

*I*F WE REALLY want a Christian society we must teach Christianity, and it is absolutely impossible to teach Christianity without teaching Christian dogma.

CC 30

Official Christianity, of late years, has been having what is known as "a bad press." We are constantly assured that the churches are empty because preachers insist too much upon doctrine—"dull dogma," as people call it. The fact is the precise opposite. It is the neglect of dogma that makes for dullness. The Christian faith is the most exciting drama that ever staggered the imagination of man— and the dogma is the drama.

CC 3

Volumes of angry controversy have been poured out about the Christian creeds, under the impression that they represent, not statements of fact, but arbitrary edicts. The conditions of salvation, for instance, are discussed as though they were conditions for membership in some fantastic club like the Red-Headed League. They do not purport to be anything of the kind. Rightly or wrongly, they purport to be necessary conditions based on the facts of human nature.

MM 15

It was said, sneeringly, by someone that if a clam could conceive of God, it would conceive of Him in the shape of a great, big clam. Naturally. And if God has revealed Himself to clams, it could only be under conditions of perfect clamhood, since any other manifestation would be wholly irrelevant to clam nature.

MM 90

It is, however, well to note that where Christianity is concerned, a total retreat from the material world is not merely heretical but impossible; for the central Christian doctrine is precisely that of God incarnate in matter, its central act of worship the bodily receiving of God's substance in the sacrament of bread and wine, and its unique eschatological expectation the Resurrection of the Flesh.

PSPS 51-52

To complain that man measures God by his own experience is a waste of time; man measures everything by his own experience; he has no other yardstick.

MM 24

Teachers and preachers never, I think, make it sufficiently clear that dogmas are not a set of arbitrary regulations invented *a priori* by a committee of theologians enjoying a bout of all-in dialectical wrestling. Most of them were hammered out under pressure of urgent practical necessity to provide an answer to heresy. And heresy is, as I have tried to show, largely the expression of opinion of the untutored average man, trying to grapple with the problems of the universe at the point where they begin to interfere with his daily life and thought.

CC 34

It is not true at all that dogma is "hopelessly irrelevant" to the life and thought of the average man. What is true is that ministers of the Christian religion often assert that it is, present it for consideration as though it were, and, in fact, by their faulty exposition of it make it so. The central dogma of the Incarnation is that by which relevance stands or falls. If Christ was only man, then He is entirely irrelevant to any thought about God; if He is only God, then He is entirely irrelevant to any experience of human life. It is, in the strictest sense, *necessary* to the salvation of relevance that a man should believe *rightly* the Incarnation of Our Lord Jesus Christ. Unless he believes rightly, there is not the faintest reason why he should believe at all. And in that case, it is wholly irrelevant to chatter about "Christian principles."

CC 32

But if Christian dogma is irrelevant to life, to what, in Heaven's name, is it relevant?—since religious dogma is in fact nothing but a statement of doctrines concerning the nature of life and the universe. If Christian ministers really believe it is only an intellectual game for theologians and has no bearing upon human life, it is no wonder that their congregations are ignorant, bored, and bewildered.

CC 31

Now, we may call Christian doctrine exhilarating or we may call it devastating; we may call it revelation or we may call it rubbish; but if we call it dull, then words have no meaning at all. That God should play the tyrant over man is a dismal story of unrelieved oppression; that man should play the tyrant over man is the usual dreary record of human futility; but that man should play the tyrant over God and find Him a better man than himself is an astonishing drama indeed. Any journalist, hearing of it for the first time, would recognize it as News; those who did hear it for the first time actually called it News, and good news at that; though we are apt to forget that the word Gospel ever meant anything so sensational.

CC 7

It would not perhaps be altogether surprising if, in this nominally Christian country, where the Creeds are daily recited, there were a number of people who knew all about Christian doctrine and disliked it. It is more startling to discover how many people there are who heartily dislike and despise Christianity without having the faintest notion what it is. If you tell them, they cannot believe you. I do not mean that they cannot believe the doctrine: that would be understandable enough, since it takes some believing. I mean that they simply cannot believe that anything so interesting, so exciting, and so dramatic can be the orthodox Creed of the Church.

CC 20

The Drama

*L*ET US, in Heaven's name, drag out the Divine Drama from under the dreadful accumulation of slipshod thinking and trashy sentiment heaped upon it, and set it on an open stage to startle the world into some sort of vigorous reaction. If the pious are the first to be shocked, so much the worse for the pious—others will pass into the Kingdom of Heaven before them. If all men are offended because of Christ, let them be offended; but where is the sense of their being offended at something that is not Christ and is nothing like Him? We do Him singularly little honour by watering down His personality till it could not offend a fly. Surely it is not the business of the Church to adapt Christ to men, but to adapt men to Christ.

CC 24

Possibly we might prefer not to take this tale too seriously —there are disquieting points about it. Here we had a man of Divine character walking and talking among us —and what did we find to do with Him? The common people, indeed, "heard Him gladly"; but our leading authorities in Church and State considered that He talked too much and uttered too many disconcerting truths. So we bribed one of His friends to hand Him over quietly to the police, and we tried Him on a rather vague charge of creating a disturbance, and had Him publicly flogged and hanged on the common gallows, "thanking God we were rid of a knave." All this was not very creditable to us, even if He was (as many people thought and think) only a harmless crazy preacher. But if the Church is right about Him, it was more discreditable still; for the man we hanged was God Almighty.

So that is the outline of the official story—the tale of the time when God was the under-dog and got beaten,

when He submitted to the conditions He had laid down
and became a man like the men He had made, and the
men He had made broke Him and killed Him. This is
the dogma we find so dull—this terrifying drama of
which God is the victim and hero.

If this is dull, then what, in Heaven's name, is worthy
to be called exciting?
                                                    CC 5

There is a dialectic in Christian sacred art which impels
it to stress, from time to time, now the eternal, and now
the temporal elements in the Divine drama. The crucifix
displays in one period the everlasting Son reigning from
the tree; in another, the human Jesus disfigured with
blood and grief.
                                          MBTK 17

The Incarnate life of God on earth, because it is a historic
fact, is at once the supreme instance and the unique natural symbol of the whole history of man, and the whole
nature of God, and the relations between them.
                                          IPD 8

For the Christian affirmation is that a number of quite
commonplace human beings, in an obscure province of
the Roman Empire, killed and murdered God Almighty
—quite casually, almost as a matter of religious and
political routine, and certainly with no notion that they
were doing anything out of the way.   *MBTK* 21

The knowledge which the British public has of the New
Testament is extensive, but in many respects peculiar.

The books are, on the whole, far better known as a collection of disjointed texts and moral aphorisms wrenched from their contexts than as a coherent history made up of coherent episodes. Most people are aware that Jesus was born at Bethlehem, and that after a short ministry of teaching and healing He was judicially murdered at Jerusalem, only to rise from the dead on the third day. But for all except the diminishing company of the instructed, the intervening period is left in the jumbled chronology of the Synoptists—a string of parables, a bunch of miracles, a discourse, a set of "sayings", a flash of apocalyptic thunder—here a little and there a little. And although many scattered fragments of teaching are commonly remembered and quoted (to the exclusion of as many more, less palatable to the taste of the times), they are remembered chiefly as detached pronouncements unrelated to the circumstances that called them forth. A multitude of people will recall that "the devil is the father of lies" for one who could state on what occasion the words were spoken and to whom, or make a precis of the argument developed in the long, pugnacious, and provocative piece of dialectic in which they occur.

MBTK 18

. . . for whatever reason God chose to make man as he is —limited and suffering and subject to sorrows and death —He had the honesty and the courage to take His own medicine. Whatever game He is playing with His creation, He has kept His own rules and played fair. He can exact nothing from man that He has not exacted from Himself.

CC 4

Creation

$\mathcal{M}$AN IS NEVER truly himself except when he is actively creating something.

BH 23

A loose and sentimental theology begets loose and sentimental art-forms.

MBTK 19

Thought is what changes knowledge into energy.

BH 20

The Church asserts that there is a Mind which made the universe, that He made it because He is the sort of Mind that takes pleasure in creation, and that if we want to know what the Mind of the Creator is, we must look at Christ. In Him, we shall discover a Mind that loved His own creation so completely that He became part of it, suffered with and for it, and made it a sharer in His own glory and a fellow-worker with Himself in the working out of His own design for it.

CC 10

Well-meaning readers who try to identify the writer with his characters or to excavate the author's personality and opinions from his books are frequently astonished by the ferocious rudeness with which the author himself salutes these efforts at reabsorbing his work into himself. They are an assault upon the independence of his creatures, which he very properly resents. Painful misunderstandings of this kind may rive the foundations of social intercourse, and produce explosions which seem quite out of proportion to their apparent causes. . . .

"I am sure Lord Peter will end up as a convinced Christian."

"From what I know of him, nothing is more unlikely."

"But as a Christian yourself, you must *want* him to be one."

"He would be horribly embarrassed by any such suggestion."

"But he's *far* too intelligent and far too nice, not to be a Christian."

"My dear lady, Peter is not the Ideal Man; he is an eighteenth-century Whig gentleman, born a little out of his time, and doubtful whether any claim to possess a soul is not a rather vulgar piece of presumption."

"I am disappointed."

"I'm afraid I can't help that."

(No; you shall *not impose either your will or mine upon my creature. He is what he is, I will work no irrelevant miracles upon him, either for propaganda, or to curry favour, or to establish the consistency of my own principles. He exists in his own right and not to please you. Hands off.)*

MM 130-131

Wimsey was unlucky. Miss Climpson was not to be found. She had had her lunch early and gone out, saying she felt that a long country walk would do her good. Mrs. Budge was rather afraid she had had some bad news— she had seemed so upset and worried since yesterday evening.

"But indeed, sir," she added, "if you was quick, you might find her up at the church. She often drops in there to say her prayers like. Not a respectful way to approach a place of worship to my mind, do you think so yourself,

sir? Popping in and out on a week-day, the same as if it
was a friend's house. And coming home from Communion as cheerful as anything and ready to laugh and
make jokes. I don't see as how we was meant to make an
ordinary thing of religion that way—so disrespectful
and nothing uplifting to the 'art about it. But there! we
all 'as our failings, and Miss Climpson is a nice lady and
that I must say, even if she is a Roaming Catholic or next
door to one."

Lord Peter thought that Roaming Catholic was rather
an appropriate name for the more ultramontane section
of the High Church party. At the moment, however, he
felt he could not afford time for religious discussion, and
set off for the church in quest of Miss Climpson.

The doors of S. Onesimus were hospitably open, and
the red Sanctuary lamp made a little spot of welcoming
brightness in the rather dark building. Coming in from
the June sunshine, Wimsey blinked a little before he
could distinguish anything else. Presently he was able to
make out a dark, bowed figure kneeling before the lamp.
For a moment he hoped it was Miss Climpson, but presently saw to his disappointment that it was merely a
Sister in a black habit, presumably taking her turn to
watch before the Host. The only other occupant of the
church was a priest in a cassock, who was busy with the
ornaments on the High Altar. It was the Feast of S. John,
Wimsey remembered suddenly. He walked up the aisle,
hoping to find his quarry hidden in some obscure corner.
His shoes squeaked. This annoyed him. It was a thing
which Bunter never permitted. He was seized with a
fancy that the squeak was produced by diabolic possession
—a protest against a religious atmosphere on the part of
his own particular besetting devil. Pleased with this
thought, he moved forward more confidently.

The priest's attention was attracted by the squeak. He
turned and came down towards the intruder. No doubt,

thought Wimsey, to offer his professional services to
exorcise the evil spirit.

"Were you looking for anybody?" inquired the priest,
courteously.

"Well, I was looking for a lady," began Wimsey.
Then it struck him that this sounded a little odd under
the circumstances, and he hastened to explain more fully,
in the stifled tones considered appropriate to consecrated
surroundings.

"Oh, yes," said the priest, quite unperturbed, "Miss
Climpson was here a little time ago, but I fancy she has
gone. Not that I usually keep tabs on my flock," he
added, with a laugh, "but she spoke to me before she
went. Was it urgent? What a pity you should have missed
her. Can I give any kind of message or help you in
any way?"

"No, thanks," said Wimsey. "Sorry to bother you. Un-
seemly to come and try to haul people out of church, but
—yes, it was rather important. I'll leave a message at the
house. Thanks frightfully."

He turned away; then stopped and came back.

"I say," he said, "you give advice on moral problems
and all that sort of thing, don't you?"

"Well, we're supposed to try," said the priest. "Is
anything bothering you in particular?"

"Ye-es," said Wimsey, "nothing religious, I don't
mean—nothing about infallibility or the Virgin Mary or
anything of that sort. Just something I'm not comfortable
about."

The priest—who was, in fact, the vicar, Mr. Tredgold
—indicated that he was quite at Lord Peter's service.

"It's very good of you. Could we come somewhere
where I didn't have to whisper so much. I never can explain things in a whisper. Sort of paralyses one, don't
you know."

"Let's go outside," said Mr. Tredgold.

So they went out and sat on a flat tombstone.

"It's like this," said Wimsey. "Hypothetical case, you see, and so on. S'posin' one knows somebody who's very, very ill and can't last long anyhow. And they're in awful pain and all that, and kept under morphia—practically dead to the world, you know. And suppose that by dyin' straight away they could make something happen which they really wanted to happen and which couldn't happen if they lived on a little longer (I can't explain exactly how, because I don't want to give personal details and so on)—you get the idea? Well, supposin' somebody who knew all that was just to give 'em a little push off so to speak—hurry matters on—why should that be a very dreadful crime?"

"The law——" began Mr. Tredgold.

"Oh, the law says it's a crime, fast enough," said Wimsey. "But do you honestly think it's very bad? I know you'd call it a sin, of course, but why is it so very dreadful? It doesn't do the person any harm, does it?"

"We can't answer that," said Mr. Tredgold, "without knowing the ways of God with the soul. In those last weeks or hours of pain and unconsciousness, the soul may be undergoing some necessary part of its pilgrimage on earth. It isn't our business to cut it short. Who are we to take life and death into our hands?"

"Well, we do it all day, one way or another. Juries—soldiers—doctors—all that. And yet I do feel, somehow, that it isn't the right thing in this case. And yet, by interfering—finding things out and so on—one may do far worse harm. Start all kinds of things."

"I think," said Mr. Tredgold, "that the sin—I won't use that word—the damage to Society, the wrongness of the thing lies much more in the harm it does the killer than in anything it can do to the person who is killed. Especially, of course, if the killing is to the killer's own advantage. The consequence you mention—this thing which the sick person wants done—does the other person stand to benefit by it, may I ask?"

"Yes. That's just it. He—she—they do."

"That puts it at once on a different plane from just hastening a person's death out of pity. Sin is in the intention, not the deed. That is the difference between divine law and human law. It is bad for a human being to get to feel that he has any right whatever to dispose of another person's life to his own advantage. It leads him on to think himself above all laws—Society is never safe from the man who has deliberately committed murder with impunity. That is why—or one reason why—God forbids private vengeance."

"You mean that one murder leads to another."

"Very often. In any case it leads to a readiness to commit others."

"It has. That's the trouble. But it wouldn't have if I hadn't started trying to find things out. Ought I to have left it alone?"

"I see. That is very difficult. Terrible, too, for you. You feel responsible."

"Yes."

"You yourself are not serving a private vengeance?"

"Oh, no. Nothing really to do with me. Started in like a fool to help somebody who'd got into trouble about the thing through having suspicions himself. And my beastly interference started the crimes all over again."

"I shouldn't be troubled. Probably the murderer's own guilty fears would have led him into fresh crimes even without your interference."

"That's true," said Wimsey, remembering Mr. Trigg.

"My advice to you is to do what you think is right, according to the laws which we have been brought up to respect. Leave the consequences to God. And try to think charitably, even of wicked people. You know what I mean. Bring the offender to justice, but remember that if we all got justice, you and I wouldn't escape either."

"I know. Knock the man down but don't dance on the body. Quite. Forgive my troublin' you—and excuse my bargin' off, because I've got a date with a friend. Thanks so much. I don't feel quite so rotten about it now. But I was gettin' worried."

Mr. Tredgold watched him as he trotted away between the graves. "Dear, dear," he said, "how nice they are. So kindly and scrupulous and so vague outside their public-school code. And much more nervous and sensitive than people think. A very difficult class to reach. I must make a special intention for him at Mass to-morrow."

Being a practical man, Mr. Tredgold made a knot in his handkerchief to remind himself of this pious resolve.

"The problem—to interfere or not to interfere— God's law and Caesar's. Policemen, now—it's no problem to them. But for the ordinary man—how hard to disentangle his own motives. I wonder what brought him here. Could it possibly be—No!" said the vicar, checking himself, "I have no right to speculate." He drew out his handkerchief again and made another mnemonic knot as a reminder against his next confession that he had fallen into the sin of inquisitiveness.

UD 225-230

Time and History

TIME HAS BEEN exercising the minds of many writers of late. It has been suggested that it is pure illusion, or at most a cross-section of eternity, and that we may be comforted for the failures of our manhood by remembering that the youthful idealists we once were are our permanent and eternal selves. This doctrine is not really even consoling; since, if our youth is co-eternal with our age, then equally, our age is co-eternal with our youth; the corruption of our ends poisons our beginnings as certainly as the purity of our beginnings sanctifies our ends. The Church has always carefully distinguished time from eternity as carefully as she has distinguished the Logos from the Father.

DTP 11 (Introd.)

War is an ugly disaster; it is not a final catastrophe. Whatever men may have said in their haste and terror, let us get that fact firmly into our heads. There are no final catastrophes. Like every other historical event, war is not an end, but a beginning.

BH 11

God, unlike even the greatest of created beings, is not subject to time.

EC 107

While time lasts there will always be a future, and that future will hold both good and evil, since the world is made to that mingled pattern.

BH 11

Something is happening to us today which has not happened for a very long time. We are waging a war of religion. Not a civil war between adherents of the same religion, but a life-and-death struggle between Christian and pagan. The Christians are, it must be confessed, not very good Christians, and the pagans do not officially proclaim themselves worshippers of Mahound or even of Odin, but the stark fact remains that Christendom and heathendom now stand face to face as they have not done in Europe since the days of Charlemagne.

CC 25

Few things are more striking than the change which has taken place during my own lifetime in the attitude of the intelligentsia towards the spokesmen of Christian opinion. When I was a child, bishops expressed doubts about the Resurrection, and were called courageous. When I was a girl, G. K. Chesterton professed belief in the Resurrection, and was called whimsical. When I was at college, thoughtful people expressed belief in the Resurrection "in a spiritual sense", and were called advanced; (any other kind of belief was called obsolete, and its professors were held to be simpleminded). When I was middle-aged, a number of lay persons, including some poets and writers of popular fiction, put forward rational arguments for the Resurrection, and were called courageous. Today, any lay apologist for Christianity, who is not a clergyman and whose works are sold and read, is liable to be abused in no uncertain terms as a mountebank, a reactionary, a tool of the Inquisition, a spiritual snob, an intellectual bully, an escapist, an obstructionist, a psychopathic introvert, an insensitive extravert, and an enemy of society. The charges are not always mutually compatible, but the common animus behind them is unmistakable, and its name is fear. Writers who attack these domineering Christians are called courageous.

PSPS 69

To-day is a historic period like any other.

Purg. 45

We cannot, after all, have it both ways. If all truths are period products, then our own standards offer no secure basis for passing judgement on those of former ages; if any truths have claims on universality, then every claim, old or new, requires to be examined on its merits.

Purg. 46

Christianity . . . outrages the tidy-minded by occupying a paradoxical position. On the one hand, it made modern science and the modern views of history possible by insisting that the pattern of events was not (as the Greek philosophers thought) static or cyclic, but a progression in time from a beginning to an end. On the other, it tiresomely maintains that at every point in the developing temporal process, the conditioned truths are referable to an extra-temporal standard of absolute truth, before which all souls enjoy complete equality, no aristocratic privilege being attached to the accident of later birth.

PSPS 72

The distinguishing marks of the mediaeval cosmos were hierarchy, order, and purpose. These were reflected in the political ideals of the day: church and state, with their ascending ranks of honour, founded upon function and status; the steady effort to bring code and canon law into conformity with natural law; the tenacious belief in the ultimate establishment of a perfect universal state that should usher in the reign of the Kingdom of God on earth. This ideal, like the cosmos upon which it

was modelled, wins little admiration from an age which
prefers equality to hierarchy, and contract to status;
which seems to have almost abandoned hope or belief
in purpose; and whose conception of order wavers between totalitarian bureaucracy and a catch-as-catch-can
individualism.   *FPD* 99

We have become antagonistic to the very idea of order—
although, rather inconsistently, we are accustomed to
put a good deal of faith in "planning".   *FPD* 42

I think it was chiefly Cyrus and Ahasuerus who prodded
me into the belated conviction that history was all of a
piece, and that the Bible was part of it. One might have
expected Jesus to provide the link between two worlds
—the Caesars were classical history all right. But Jesus
was a special case. One used a particular tone of voice in
speaking of Him, and He dressed neither like Bible
nor like classics—He dressed like Jesus, in a fashion
closely imitated (down to the halo) by His disciples. If
He belonged anywhere, it was to Rome, in spite of
strenuous prophetic efforts to identify Him with the
story of the Bible Jews. Indeed the Jews themselves had
undergone a mysterious change in the blank pages between the Testaments: in the Old, they were "good"
people; in the New, they were "bad" people—it seemed
doubtful whether they really were the same people.
Nevertheless, Old or New, all these people lived in
Church and were "Bible characters"—they were not real
in the sense that King Alfred was a real person; still less
could their conduct be judged by standards that applied
to one's own contemporaries.   *UO* 24

We are so much accustomed to viewing the whole
[Christian] story from a post-Resurrection, and indeed
from a post-Nicene, point of view, that we are apt, without realising it, to attribute to all the New Testament
characters the same kind of detailed theological awareness which we have ourselves. We judge their behaviour
as though all of them—disciples, Pharisees, Romans,
and men-in-the-street—had known with Whom they
were dealing and what the meaning of all the events actually was. But they did not know it. The disciples had
only the foggiest inkling of it, and nobody else came
anywhere near grasping what it was all about. If the
Chief Priests and the Roman Governor had been aware
that they were engaged in crucifying God—if Herod the
Great had ordered his famous massacre with the express
intention of doing away with God—then they would
have been quite exceptionally and diabolically wicked
people. And indeed, we like to think that they were: it
gives us a reassuring sensation that "it can't happen
here". And to this comfortable persuasion we are as-
sisted by the stately and ancient language of the Author-
ised Version, and by the general air of stained-glass-
window decorum with which the tale is usually presented to us. The characters are not men and women:
they are all "sacred personages", standing about in sym-
bolic attitudes, and self-consciously awaiting the fulfil-
ment of prophecies.

MBTK 22

If life can be made worthwhile, death will not matter at
all; for life can be good, but it is not and cannot be an
absolute, any more than anything else in this world. To
make life into an absolute is to exchange it for death-
in-life, because, like every other temporal absolute, life
takes revenge on those who make it a god.

BH 135

I have never yet heard any middle-aged man or woman who worked with his or her brains express any regret for the passing of youth.

BH 25

Nothing is more cruel to the young than to tell them that the world is made for youth.

BH 26

During the last fifty years or thereabouts we have come to believe that the basis of all love is sexual, and that therefore any and every love which does not issue in sexual satisfactions is warped in its nature and in its effects. And by our belief we make it so, for we bring to bear upon the unfortunate lover all the relentless one-sided pressure of our current critical assumptions. But when Dante loved it was otherwise. The denial of a physical desire was not then looked upon as a solecism, nor had the achievement of happiness been erected into a moral obligation. The lover who had set his heart upon the unattainable suffered, no doubt, the usual bodily frustrations, but he was not haunted by a guilty sense of personal failure and social inadequacy. He was not despised as an escapist; nobody told him that he was maladjusted, or hinted that there was something seriously wrong with him if he was not uproariously releasing his repressions at every turn. On the contrary, he was admired and commended. Whatever his private distresses, he could feel that his public conduct was irreproachable. He was sustained by his whole culture.

Purg. 43

Truth and Reality

*T*HE PROPER question to be asked about any creed is not, "Is it pleasant?" but, "Is it true?"

MM 16

Those who make it a reproach to Christianity that it taught no new morality and invented no new kind of Deity could not be more laughably wide of the mark. What it did was to guarantee that the old morality was actually valid, and the old beliefs literally true.

MBTK 28

If we refuse assent to reality: if we rebel against the nature of things and choose to think that what we at the moment want is the centre of the universe to which everything else ought to accommodate itself, the first effect on us will be that the whole universe will seem to be filled with an implacable and inexplicable hostility. We shall begin to feel that everything has a down on us, and that, being so badly treated, we have a just grievance against things in general. That is the knowledge of good as evil and the fall into illusion. If we cherish and fondle that grievance, and would rather wallow in it and vent our irritation in spite and malice than humbly admit we are in the wrong and try to amend our behaviour so as to get back to reality, that is, while it lasts, the deliberate choice, and a foretaste of the experience, of Hell.

IPD 64

God in Heaven—is the only unconditioned reality. All other reality is derived from God, being either immediately created by Him, or engendered or evolved or

manufactured by the mediation of His creatures, inter-
acting among themselves.   *IPD* 47

"I, Mary, am the fact; God is the truth; but Jesus is fact
and truth—he is reality. You cannot see the immortal
truth till it is born in the flesh of the fact. And because all
birth is a sundering of the flesh, fact and reality seem to
go separate ways. But it is not really so; the feet that
must walk this road were made of me. Only one Jesus is
to die today—one person whom you know—the truth
of God and the fact of Mary. This is reality. From the
beginning of time until now, this is the only thing that
has ever really happened. When you understand this
you will understand all prophecies, and all history. . . ."
                    MBTK 295 (Play XI, Scene I)

. . . the fashionable habit of calling the prohibition of
the Fruit of Knowledge an "arbitrary taboo" is a quite
unjustifiable travesty of the Bible story. There, God is
represented as saying to Adam and Eve: "Do not eat:
if you do, it will kill you"—and I do not know what else
one could reasonably say to anybody when begging him
to refrain from taking strychnine or prussic acid.
                    IPD 63

The popular mind has grown so confused that it is no
longer able to receive any statement of fact except as an
expression of personal feeling.   *MM* ix

At that first Great Synod of East and West, the Church
declared her mind as to the Nature of Him whom she
worshipped. By the insertion of a single word in the

baptismal symbol of her faith, she affirmed that That which had been Incarnate at Bethlehem in the reign of Augustus Caesar, suffered under Pontius Pilate, and risen from death in the last days of Tiberius, was neither deified man, nor angel, nor demi-god, nor any created being however exalted, but Very God of Very God, co-equal and co-eternal with the Father.

EC 5 (Introd.)

In ordinary times we get along surprisingly well, on the whole, without ever discovering what our faith really is. If, now and again, this remote and academic problem is so unmannerly as to thrust its way into our minds, there are plenty of things we can do to drive the intruder away. We can get the car out, or go to a party or the cinema, or read a detective story, or have a row with the district council, or write a letter to the papers about the habits of the night-jar or Shakespeare's use of nautical metaphor. Thus we build up a defence mechanism against self-questioning, because, to tell the truth, we are very much afraid of ourselves.

UO 14

. . . it is hardly an exaggeration to say that many people contrive never once to think for themselves from the cradle to the grave. They may go through the motions of thinking, but in fact they solve all problems either by the dictate of their emotions, or by accepting without enquiry the ruling of some outside authority. Even quite well-informed people do this.

BH 19

To discover (as I have before now discovered) that some enquirer is "*so* much interested in what you say about Christianity," but has never so much as taken the trouble to read the Gospels, is the kind of thing that makes one despair of the rational intelligence.

BH 117

. . . the doctrine of the immortality of the soul, though Christians do in fact believe it, is not particularly characteristic of Christianity, nor even vital to it. No Christian creed so much as mentions it, and theoretically, it would be quite compatible with Christian belief if soul as well as body had to undergo the experience of death. The characteristic belief of Christendom is in the Resurrection of the Body and the life everlasting of the complete body-soul complex. Excessive spirituality is the mark, not of the Christian, but of the Gnostic.

FPD 93

. . . there is a fundamental error about the Church's attitude to the Active Life—a persistent assumption that Catholic Christianity, like any Oriental gnosticism, despises the flesh and enjoins a complete detachment from all secular activities. Such a view is altogether heretical. No religion that centres about a Divine Incarnation can take up such an attitude as that. What the Church enjoins is quite different: namely, that all the good things of this world are to be loved because God loves them, as God loves them, for the love of God, and for no other reason.

IPD 113

It is significant that readers should so often welcome the detective-story as a way of escape from the problems of existence. It "takes their mind off their troubles." Of

course it does; for it softly persuades them that love and
hatred, poverty and unemployment, finance and inter-
national politics, are problems capable of being dealt
with and solved in the same manner as Death in the
Library.

MM 188-189

"There's nothing you can't prove if your outlook is only
sufficiently limited."

WB 88

Evil

*G*OD DID NOT abolish the fact of evil: He transformed it. He did not stop the crucifixion: He rose from the dead.

GDS 43

We must abandon any idea that we are the slaves of chance, or environment, or our subconscious; any vague notion that good and evil are merely relative terms, or that conduct and opinion do not really matter; any comfortable persuasion that, however shiftlessly we muddle through life, it will somehow or other all come right on the night. We must try to believe that man's will is free, that he can consciously exercise choice, and that his choice can be decisive to all eternity.

Hell 11

How often does a man know the precise moment when his will consented to sin? By what obscure interior resolution did the thought, "I wish my brother were dead" give place to the settled intention: "I mean to murder him"? or the speculative premeditation of murder become a foregone conclusion, crystallising into an act? . . . As a rule, the assent of evil is not recognised until after it has been ratified by the conscious mind.

IPD 133

When a child falls over a chair, its instant reaction will very likely be to say, "Naughty chair", and belabour it soundly with whatever first comes to hand. That is apt to strike the grown-up Adam, who knows more than the child about the nature of inanimate matter, as funny: but if Adam is sensible he will take the stick away and

not encourage the child to expect the material universe
to accommodate itself to his wishes.

The grown-up Adam, having laughed at the child,
may then go to Piccadilly Tube Station with the intention of taking a train to Stanmore. With his mind fixed
on the Test Match or the sins of the Government, he
may neglect to consult the indicator which is saying
plainly that the train now at the platform is going to
Watford, and when, having passed Baker Street in a
fond illusion, he looks up at the next station and finds
that it is not St. John's Wood, but Marylebone, he will
mutter savagely that he has got into "the wrong train".
Neither will it for a moment occur to him that what he
is saying is as absurd as what the child said. But what is
wrong with the train? In the eyes of God and London
Passenger Transport, it is a perfectly good train, pro-
ceeding on its lawful occasions to the destination appointed for it by a superior power. To be sure, it has got
a wrong passenger, who has nobody to blame but himself. But the determination to see the good as evil and
the right train as a wrong 'un has entrenched itself in
the very core of Adam's language: and it is well for his
soul if he confines himself to that merely conventional
method of transferring his own errors to the universe,
and does not angrily add that "all these damned trains
seem to go to Watford".   *IPD* 64

The timid Christian, and even—perhaps even especially
—the corrupt Christian, knows more about the intimate
processes of pure evil than any professor of humanism
can ever do.   *IPD* 173

The thing that Liberal Humanism finds it most difficult
to understand or cope with is the riddle of the evil mind,

practising a purposeless malignity for its own sake. The love of evil is sub-rational, as the Divine charity is super-rational; and the golden mean of reason is as incapable of the one as of the other.

FPD 71

Humanism is always apt to underestimate, and to be baffled by, the deliberate will to evil. Neither is it any sure protection against heresy.

Hell 120

. . . evil can never be undone, but only purged and redeemed.

EC 181

We are reminded of the old lady who rebuked someone for saying "What the devil——!" on the ground that "she did not like to hear him speak so flippantly about a sacred personage".

IPD 26

. . . one of the most important things we have to do is to distinguish the Devil as (in the sight of God) he is, and the thing which may be called the "diabolic set-up". The underlying actuality is miserable, hideous, and squalid; the "set-up" is the facade which the Devil shows to the world—and a very noble facade it often is, and the nobler, the more dangerous. The Devil is a spiritual lunatic, but, like many lunatics, he is extremely plausible and cunning. His brain is, so to speak, in perfectly good working order except for that soft and corrupted spot in the centre, where dwells the eternal illusion. His method of working is to present us with the magnificent set-up, hoping we shall not use either our brains or our spiritual faculties to penetrate the illusion. He is playing for sympathy; therefore he is much better served by exploiting our virtues than by appealing to our lower passions; consequently, it is when the Devil looks most noble and reasonable that he is most dangerous.

PSPS 231

The devils are fallen angels. Satan and his followers chose the not-God, and when they had it, they found that it was hell. In that obduracy they suffer; and into that suffering they endeavour to drag the rest of creation—of which man in particular concerns us. Their whole will is to hatred and negation and destruction, and if they could accomplish that will wholly they would be none the happier, since happiness is not in them—they have destroyed their own capacity for happiness. The lust for destruction in no way increases the happiness of those who indulge in it—if anything, the more successful they are in it, the more miserable they are—but they persist in it because they have destroyed their own will for anything else. This is, of course, a witless state of mind; but then the intellect is one of the first things that the evil will destroys. That it is not an impossible state of mind is quite apparent—for we can see it existing in human beings today—and sometimes can find it only too clearly in our virtuous selves: for example, in jealousy that searches avidly for fresh occasions of the distrust which torments it: or in our savage resentment against those we have injured, which prompts us to renew the injury and so increase the miserable resentment.

PSPS 231

(Mephistopheles speaks:)
"I am the price that all things pay for being,
The shadow on the world, thrown by the world
Standing in its own light, which light God is."

DTP 138 (Scene IV)

. . . none of us feels the true love of God till we realize
how wicked we are. But you can't teach people that—
they have to learn by experience.

EC 101

We shall not, of course, go so far as to say that evil is
ever good in itself, but only that it can, in every sense of
the words, "be made good." This is a view of the matter
in which the Christian religion has, so to speak, specialised. It would no doubt have been well if the world had
altogether refrained from evil; yet, the evil having oc-
curred, the opportunity appears to make out of that evil
a still more noble good; the second Adam is greater than
the first Adam could ever have been.

BH 15-16

Sin

$\mathcal{P}$ERHAPS the bitterest commentary on the way in which Christian doctrine has been taught in the last few centuries is the fact that to the majority of people the word "immorality" has come to mean one thing and one thing only. By a hideous irony, our shrinking reprobation of that sin has made us too delicate so much as to name it, so that we have come to use for it the words which were made to cover the whole range of human corruption. A man may be greedy and selfish; spiteful, cruel, jealous, and unjust; violent and brutal; grasping, unscrupulous, and a liar; stubborn and arrogant; stupid, morose, and dead to every noble instinct—and still we are ready to say of him that he is not an immoral man. I am reminded of a young man who once said to me with perfect simplicity: "I did not know there were seven deadly sins: please tell me the names of the other six."

CC 63

THE SEVEN DEADLY SINS

Pride. Pride *(Superbia)* is the head and root of all sin, both original and actual. It is the endeavour to be "as God," making self, instead of God, the centre about which the will and desire revolve.

Purg. 147

Envy. The sin of Envy *(Invidia)* differs from that of Pride in that it contains always an element of fear. The proud man is self-sufficient, rejecting with contempt the notion that anybody can be his equal or superior. The envious man is afraid of losing something by the admission of superiority in others, and therefore looks with grudging hatred upon other men's gifts and good fortune, taking every opportunity to run them down or deprive them of their happiness.

Purg. 170

Wrath. The effect of Wrath *(Ira)* is to blind the judgement and to suffocate the natural feelings and responses, so that a man does not know what he is doing.

Purg. 192

Sloth. The sin which in English is called Sloth *(Accidia* or *Acedia)* is insidious, and assumes such Protean shapes that it is rather difficult to define. It is not merely idleness of mind and laziness of body: it is that whole poisoning of the will which, beginning with indifference and an attitude "I couldn't care less," extends to the deliberate refusal of joy and culminates in morbid introspection and despair. One form of it which appeals very much to some modern minds is that acquiescence in evil and error which readily disguises itself as "Tolerance"; another is that refusal to be moved by the contemplation of the good and beautiful which is known as "Disillusionment," and sometimes as "Knowledge of the World"; yet another is that withdrawal into an "ivory tower" of Isolation which is the peculiar temptation of the artist and the contemplative, and is popularly called "Escapism."

Purg. 209

Covetousness. Covetousness *(Avaritia)* is the inordinate love of wealth, and the power that wealth gives, whether it is manifested by miserly hoarding or by lavish spending. It is a peculiarly earth-bound sin, looking to nothing beyond the rewards of this life.

Purg. 221

Gluttony. The sin of Gluttony *(Gula)* is—specifically—an undue attention to the pleasures of the palate, whether by sheer excess in eating and drinking, or by the opposite fault of fastidiousness. More generally, it includes all over-indulgence in bodily comforts—the concentration, whether jovial or fretful, on a "high standard of living."

Purg. 251

Lust. Lust [*Luxuria*] is a type of *shared* sin; at its best, and so long as it remains a sin of incontinence only, there is mutuality in it and exchange: although, in fact, mutual indulgence only serves to push both parties along the road to Hell, it is not, in intention, wholly selfish.

Hell 101

The Puritan assumption that all action disagreeable to the doer is *ipso facto* more meritorious than enjoyable action, is firmly rooted in this exaggerated valuation set on pride. I do not mean that there is no nobility in doing unpleasant things from a sense of duty, but only that there is more nobility in doing them gladly out of sheer love of the job. The Puritan thinks otherwise; he is inclined to say, "Of course, So-and-so works very hard and has given up a good deal for such-and-such a cause, but there's no merit in that—he enjoys it." The merit, of course, lies precisely in the enjoyment, and the nobility of So-and-so consists in the very fact that he is the kind of person to whom the doing of that piece of work is delightful.

MM 134

To pray when one ought to be working is as much a sin as to work when one ought to be praying.

Purg. 124

Eden is, and was always meant to be, a starting-place and not a stopping-place.

Purg. 294

If spiritual pastors are to refrain from saying anything that might ever, by any possibility, be misunderstood by anybody, they will end—as in fact many of them do— by never saying anything worth hearing. Incidentally, this particular brand of timidity is the besetting sin of the good churchman. Not that the Church approves it. She knows it of old for a part of the great, sprawling, drowsy, deadly Sin of Sloth—a sin from which the preachers of fads, schisms, heresies and anti-Christ are most laudably free.

GDS 26-27

There is a good deal to be said for the opinion that a sin is a sin and an error an error; that both should be examined, admitted, repented of, and then put out of our thoughts. Repentance is, in fact, another way of saying that the bad past is to be considered as the starting-point for better things. We bungled the last opportunity; very

well. Let us admit that and try to do better with the
new one.

BH 13-14

"Shall we," asks St. Paul, "continue in sin that grace
may abound? God forbid" (*Rom.* vi, I). The reason is
obvious; grace abounds only when there is genuine repentance, and we cannot, as the logical demon so rightly
observes (*Inf.* xxvii, 118-20), simultaneously will sin
and repentance, since this involves a contradiction in
terms.

Incidentally, a similar logical fallacy attends all inge-
nious proposals to "test the efficacy of prayer" by (for
example) praying for the patients in Ward A of a hos-
pital and leaving Ward B unprayed for, in order to see
which set recovers. Prayer undertaken in that spirit is
not prayer at all, and it requires a singular naivety to imagine that Omniscience could be so easily bamboozled.

Purg. 68-69 note

The Church says Covetousness is a deadly sin—but does
she really think so? Is she ready to found Welfare Societies to deal with financial immorality as she does with
sexual immorality? Do the officials stationed at church
doors in Italy to exclude women with bare arms turn
anybody away on the grounds that they are too well-
dressed to be honest? Do the vigilance committees who
complain of "suggestive" books and plays make any
attempt to suppress the literature which "suggests" that
getting on in the world is the chief object in life? Is
Dives, like Magdalen, ever refused the sacraments on
the grounds that he, like her, is an "open and notorious
evil-liver"? Does the Church arrange services with

bright congregational singing, for Total Abstainers from
Usury?

CC 73

When we demand justice, it is always justice on our be-
half against other people. Nobody, I imagine, would
ever ask for justice to be done *upon* him for every thing
he ever did wrong. We do not want justice—we want
revenge: and that is why, when justice is done upon us,
we cry out that God is vindictive.

IPD 67

Recent psychological research, together with a number
of other contributory factors, has influenced us to empha-
sise—possibly to over-emphasise—the importance of the
unconscious in determining our actions and opinions.
Our confidence in such faculties as will and judgment
has been undermined, and in collapsing has taken with
it a good deal of our interest in ourselves as responsible
individuals.

IPD 2

The Middle Ages had practically no psychology of the
sub-conscious. They were not altogether unaware of the
existence of the dim regions beneath the threshold; but
they were not interested. This was in a way unfortunate;
for it involved them in much speculation about the trans-
mission of hereditary guilt which an examination of the
sub-conscious might have cleared up. The examination
was eventually undertaken by a generation of scientists
to whom the whole concept of original sin had become
alien; and its results were received rather with alarm
than alacrity by a Church which had lost her eager medi-

aeval curiosity, and did not quite realise that a new
argument for her traditional truth had actually been
presented to her.

FPD 93

I remember, years ago, being engaged in correspondence
with a young man who was extremely enthusiastic about
the psychology of the unconscious, and who insisted that
the urge which issued in the writing of a story about a
murder and the urge which issued in the committing of
a murder were one and the same urge, with no difference
between them. I was writing murder-stories at the time
and may have been prejudiced, but I objected that it did
seem to me as though there must be a slight difference
of some kind somewhere, since the results were so different. I added that society in general must be aware of the
difference, since it rewarded the one result with royalties
and the other with the gallows.

IPD 4

"Why doesn't God smite this dictator dead?" is a question a little remote from us. Why, madam, did He not
strike you dumb and imbecile before you uttered that
baseless and unkind slander the day before yesterday?
Or me, before I behaved with such cruel lack of consideration to that well-meaning friend? And why, sir, did
He not cause your hand to rot off at the wrist before you
signed your name to that dirty little bit of financial
trickery?

GDS 29-30

SO LONG AS the will truly intends penitence and amendment, the Christian need not, and should not, be unduly troubled about the involuntary aberrations of the unconscious, but should simply commend the matter to God, in the confident assurance that it will be taken care of.

Purg. 130

I think that the perpetual arguments about penal systems and methods of dealing with crime would be greatly illuminated if it could be clearly grasped that the important thing in every case is to induce the criminal to *accept judgment*. If that point can be gained, then the whole distinction between ameliorative and retributive punishment tends to disappear; for the culprit then understands that the penalty is the opportunity offered to him to purge the *reatus* [his condition as an accused person] and by so doing to put himself back into right relations with society. But society, on the other hand, must be willing to take him back.

IPD 84

Every man's innocence belongs to Christ, and Christ's to him. And innocence alone can pardon without injustice, because it has paid the price.

EC 182

. . . while God does not, and man dare not, demand repentance as a condition for *bestowing* pardon, repentance remains an essential condition for *receiving* it. Hence the Church's twofold insistence—first that re-

Forgiveness

pentance is necessary, and secondly that all sin is pardoned instantly in the mere fact of the sinner's repentance. Nobody has to sit about being humiliated in the outer office while God dispatches important business, before condescending to issue a stamped official discharge accompanied by an improving lecture. Like the Father of the Prodigal Son, God can see repentance coming a great way off and is there to meet it, and the repentance is the reconciliation.

UO 10-11

It may be easier to understand what forgiveness is, if we first clear away misconceptions about what it does. It does not wipe out the consequences of the sin. The words and images used for forgiveness in the New Testament frequently have to do with the cancellation of a debt: and it is scarcely necessary to point out that when a debt is cancelled, this does not mean that the money is miraculously restored from nowhere. It means only that the obligation originally due from the borrower is voluntarily discharged by the lender. If I injure you and you mulct me in damages, then I bear the consequences; if you forbear to prosecute, then you bear the consequences. If the injury is irreparable, and you are vindictive, injury is added to injury; if you are forgiving and I am repentant, then we share the consequences and gain a friendship. But in every case the consequences are borne by somebody. The Parable of the Unmerciful Servant adds a further illuminating suggestion: that forgiveness is not merely a mutual act, but a social act. If injuries are not forgiven all round, the grace of pardon is made ineffective, and the inexorable judgment of the Law is forced into operation.

UO 9-10

. . . the blessed "joyously forgive themselves"—a thing, as we all know, extremely difficult in this life, because pride gets in the way. For instance—that dreadfully silly and unkind thing you said to poor Miss Smith when you were quite a child. Even after all these years, it makes you turn hot and writhe on your pillow if you remember it suddenly in the middle of the night; and the fact that Miss Smith was so decent about it makes you feel all the worse. But in Heaven, when you have purged off the sin, you will remember the wretched little episode only as a *fact:* you will be free for ever from the ugly shame that is the protest of your pride against being humiliated in your own eyes; and seeing Miss Smith as God sees her, you will rejoice in her beautiful charity as though it had been something else, and not your unthinking cruelty, that called it forth.

IPD 60

Morality

*I*T IS WORSE than useless for Christians to talk about the importance of Christian morality, unless they are prepared to take their stand upon the fundamentals of Christian theology. It is a lie to say that dogma does not matter; it matters enormously. It is fatal to let people suppose that Christianity is only a mode of feeling; it is vitally necessary to insist that it is first and foremost a rational explanation of the universe. It is hopeless to offer Christianity as a vaguely idealistic aspiration of a simple and consoling kind; it is, on the contrary, a hard, tough, exacting, and complex doctrine, steeped in a drastic and uncompromising realism. And it is fatal to imagine that everybody knows quite well what Christianity is and needs only a little encouragement to practise it. The brutal fact is that in this Christian country not one person in a hundred has the faintest notion what the Church teaches about God or man or society or the person of Jesus Christ.

CC 28

CHRISTIAN MORALITY

Setting aside the scandal caused by His Messianic claims and His reputation as a political firebrand, only two accusations of personal depravity seem to have been brought against Jesus of Nazareth. First, that He was a Sabbath-breaker. Secondly, that He was "a gluttonous man and a winebibber, a friend of publicans and sinners"—or (to draw aside the veil of Elizabethan English which makes it all sound so much more respectable) that He ate too heartily, drank too freely, and kept very disreputable company, including grafters of the lowest type and ladies who were no better than they should be.

For nineteen and a half centuries, the Christian

Churches have laboured, not without success, to remove this unfortunate impression made by their Lord and Master. They have hustled the Magdalens from the Communion-table, founded Total Abstinence Societies in the name of Him who made the water wine, and added improvements of their own, such as various bans and anathemas upon dancing and theatre-going. They have transferred the Sabbath from Saturday to Sunday, and, feeling that the original commandment "thou shalt not work" was rather half-hearted, have added to it a new commandment, "thou shalt not play."

Whether these activities are altogether in the spirit of Christ we need not argue. One thing is certain: that they have produced some very curious effects upon our language. They have, for example, succeeded in placing a strangely restricted interpretation on such words as "virtue," "purity" and "morality." There are a great many people now living in the world who firmly believe that "Christian morals," as distinct from purely secular morality, consist in three things and three things only: Sunday observance, not getting intoxicated, and not practising—well, in fact, not practising "immorality." I do not say that the Churches themselves would agree with this definition; I say only that this is the impression they have contrived to give the world, and that the remarkable thing about it is its extreme unlikeness to the impression produced by Christ.

Now, I do not suggest that the Church does wrong to pay attention to the regulation of bodily appetites and the proper observance of holidays. What I do suggest is that by over-emphasising this side of morality, to the comparative neglect of others, she has not only betrayed her mission but, incidentally, defeated her own aims even about "morality." She has, in fact, made an alliance with Caesar, and Caesar, having used her for his own purposes, has now withdrawn his support—for that is

Caesar's pleasant way of behaving. For the last three hundred years or so, Caesar has been concerned to maintain a public order based upon the rights of private property: consequently, he has had a vested interest in "morality." Strict morals make for the stability of family life and the orderly devolution of property, and Caesar (namely, the opinion of highly placed and influential people) has been delighted that the Church should do the work of persuading the citizen to behave accordingly. Further, a drunken workman is a bad workman, and thriftless extravagance is bad for business; therefore, Caesar has welcomed the encouragement of the Church for those qualities which make for self-help in industry. As for Sunday observance, the Church could have that if she liked, so long as it did not interfere with trade. To work all round the week ends in diminishing production; the one day in seven was necessary, and what the Church chose to do with it was no affair of Caesar's.

Unhappily, however, this alliance for mutual benefit between Church and Caesar has not lasted. The transfer of property from the private owner to the public trust or limited company enables Caesar to get on very well without personal morals and domestic stability; the conception that the consumer exists for the sake of production has made extravagance and thriftless consumption a commercial necessity: consequently, Caesar no longer sees eye to eye with the Church about these matters, and will as soon encourage a prodigal frivolity on Sunday as on any other day of the week. Why not? Business is business. The Church, shocked and horrified, is left feebly protesting against Caesar's desertion, and denouncing a "relaxation of moral codes," in which the heedless world is heartily aided and abetted by the State. The easy path of condemning what Caesar condemns or is not concerned to defend has turned out to be like the elusive garden-path in *Through the Looking-Glass;* just when one seemed to be getting somewhere, it gave itself a little shake and one found oneself walking in the opposite direction.

Now, if we look at the Gospels with the firm intention to discover the *emphasis* of Christ's morality, we shall find that it did not lie at all along the lines laid down by the opinion of highly placed and influential people. Disreputable people who knew they were disreputable were gently told to "go and sin no more"; the really unparliamentary language was reserved for those thrifty, respectable, and sabbatarian citizens who enjoyed Caesar's approval and their own. And the one and only thing that ever seems to have roused the "meek and mild" Son of God to a display of outright physical violence was precisely the assumption that "business was business." The money-changers in Jerusalem drove a very thriving trade, and made as shrewd a profit as any other set of brokers who traffic in foreign exchange; but the only use Christ had for these financiers was to throw their property down the front steps of the Temple.

Perhaps if the Churches had had the courage to lay their emphasis where Christ laid it, we might not have come to this present frame of mind in which it is assumed that the value of all work, and the value of all people, is to be assessed in terms of economics. We might not so readily take for granted that the production of anything (no matter how useless or dangerous) is justified so long as it issues in increased profits and wages; that so long as a man is well paid, it does not matter whether his work is worth-while in itself or good for his soul; that so long as a business deal keeps on the windy side of the law, we need not bother about its ruinous consequences to society or the individual. Or at any rate, now that we have seen the chaos of bloodshed which follows upon economic chaos, we might at least be able to listen with more confidence to the voice of an untainted and undivided Christendom. Doubtless it would have needed courage to turn Dives from the church-door along with Mary Magdalen; (has any prosperously fraudulent banker, I wonder, ever been refused Communion on the grounds that he was, in the words of the English Prayer-book, "an open and notorious evil liver"?) But lack of courage, and appeasement in the face of well-organised iniquity, does nothing to avert catastrophe or to secure respect.

In the list of those Seven Deadly Sins which the Church officially recognises there is the sin which is sometimes called Sloth, and sometimes Accidie. The one name is obscure to us; the other is a little misleading. It does not mean lack of hustle: it means the slow sapping of all the faculties by indifference, and by the sensation that life is pointless and meaningless, and not-worthwhile. It is, in fact, the very thing which has been called the Disease of Democracy. It is the child of Covetousness, and the parent of those other two sins which the Church calls Lust and Gluttony. Covetousness breaks down the standards by which we assess our spiritual values, and causes us to look for satisfactions in this world. The next step is the sloth of mind and body, the emptiness of heart, which destroys energy and purpose and issues in that general attitude to the universe which the interwar jazz musicians aptly named "the Blues." For the cure of the Blues, Caesar (who has his own axe to grind) prescribes the dreary frivolling which the Churches and respectable people have agreed to call "immorality," and which, in these days, is as far as possible from the rollicking enjoyment of bodily pleasures which, rightly considered, are sinful only by their excess. The mournful and medical aspect assumed by "immorality" in the present age is a sure sign that in trying to cure these particular sins we are patching up the symptoms instead of tackling the disease at its roots.

To these facts it is only fair to say that the Churches are at last waking up. The best Christian minds are making very strenuous efforts to readjust the emphasis and to break the alliance with Caesar. The chief danger is lest the Churches, having for so long acquiesced in the exploiting of the many by the few, should now think to adjust the balance by helping on the exploitation of the few by the many, instead of attacking the false standards by which everybody, rich and poor alike, has now come to assess the value of life and work. If the Churches make this mistake, they will again be merely following the shift of power from one class of the community to the other and deserting the dying Caesar to enlist the support of his successor. A more equal distribution of wealth is a good and desirable thing, but it can scarcely be attained, and cannot certainly be maintained unless we get rid of the superstition that acquisitiveness is a virtue and that the value of anything is represented in terms of profit and cost.

The Churches are justifiably shocked when the glamour of a film actress is assessed by the number of her love affairs and divorces; they are less shocked when the glamour of a man, or of a work of art, is headlined in dollars. They are shocked when "unfortunates" are reduced to selling their bodies; they are less shocked when journalists are reduced to selling their souls. They are shocked when good food is wasted by riotous living; they are less shocked when good crops are wasted and destroyed because of over-production and under-consumption. Something has gone wrong with the emphasis; and it is becoming very evident that until that emphasis is readjusted, the economic balance-sheet of the world will have to be written in blood.

Christians (surprising as it may appear) are not the only
people who fail to act up to their creed; for what deter-
minist, when his breakfast bacon is uneatable, will not
blame the free will of the cook, like any Christian?

GDS 32-33

I believe peace is one of those things, like happiness,
which we are sure to miss if we aim at them directly.

BH 134

$\mathcal{T}$HE LOSS of the doctrine [of Purgatory] has been a great loss in understanding and charity and has tended to destroy our sense of the communion between the blessed dead and ourselves.

IPD 75

It is, of course, open to anyone to say that the whole idea [of Purgatory] is morbid and exaggerated—open even to those who think nothing of queueing for twenty-four hours in acute discomfort to see the first night of a musical comedy which lasts three hours at most, which they are not sure of liking when they get there, and which they could see any other night with no trouble at all. Heaven offers only joy eternal and inexhaustible, and offers it once and for all. It is a question of value and proportion.

Purg. 21

Purgatory is not an eternal state but a temporal process, continuous with, and of a quality comparable to, our experience in this world.

IPD 74

If you insist on having your own way, you will get it. Hell is the enjoyment of your own way forever. If you really want God's way for you, you will get it in Heaven, and the pains of Purgatory will not deter you, they will be welcomed as the means to that end.

Purg. 16

When all the penitence and all the purgation are done, in this world and the next, where exactly does mankind find itself? The answer—a disappointing one perhaps for those who make a fetish of progress—is that it finds itself exactly where it originally set out from. Like Chesterton's traveller who went all round the world to discover England, man has journeyed through the troubles of Earth and the vision of Hell and the steep ascents of Purgatory simply to come home. His relationship with God is restored, he has recovered the primal innocence, he stands where the First Adam stood; Paradise is regained. Not quite as it would have been if Adam had never wished to know good and evil, for with God nothing is ever lost or wasted. The innocence is now enriched by all the bitter experience; the evil is not simply blotted out, it is redeemed. But the will, which throughout its temporal probation has been thwarted and hampered and terrified and tyrannised over by the disorderly lusts to which it enslaved itself, and which has had in consequence to be put in subjection to the Law, is now free. It can go to its own true place as swiftly and certainly as the stone falls downward or the fire mounts upward. . . . It can do what it likes, for it cannot but like what it ought.

IPD 93

. . . the soul in Purgatory has not injured God in the sense of having damaged Him or taken anything from Him: nor can he benefit God by giving Him anything, since all he has is God's already, and God wants for nothing. The only way in which the soul can injure or "grieve" God is by injuring itself; and the only thing it can restore to God is itself. It can only restore itself and purge the stain, which is the separation from God, by accepting judgment and gladly submitting to have the stain scoured off it by any means however painful: and this "cleansing of the filth," as Dante calls it, *is* itself the making of the satisfaction. In that moment of illumination which is given to it at death, the soul says, as it were:

"Lord, I see You and I see myself; I am dirty and disgusting; even though in Your infinite goodness You were ready to receive me as I am, I should not be fit to stand in Your presence and my eyes could not bear to look at You. Please clean me—I don't mind what You do to me—I'll go through fire and water, anything, to be more like what You want me to be."

IPD 80

Hell and Heaven

*I*T IS the deliberate choosing to remain in illusion and to see God and the universe as hostile to one's ego that is of the very essence of Hell. The dreadful moods when we hug our hatred and misery and are too proud to let them go are foretastes in time of what Hell eternally is. So long as we are in time and space, we can still, by God's grace and our own wills assenting, repent of Hell and come out of it. But if we carry that determination and that choice through the gates of death into the state in which there is, literally, no time, what then? Death, which was the bitter penalty attached to man's knowledge of evil, is also man's privilege and opportunity. He is not allowed just to slip away easily, body and soul, into eternity, as the early Fathers imagined he might have done if he had never lost his innocence. In knowing evil, Man had to know death as a crisis—the sharp sundering of mortal and immortal—and in that crisis he sees his choice between reality and illusion. As it passes out of the flesh the soul sees God and sees its own sin. This crisis and confrontation are technically known as the Particular Judgment. If, in the very moment of that crisis, the true self is still alive, however feebly: if, deep down beneath all perversities of selfwill, the absolute will is still set towards God's reality, and the soul can find it in itself, even at that last moment, to accept judgment—to fling away the whole miserable illusion and throw itself upon truth, then it is safe. It will have to do in Purgatory, with incredible toil and without the assistance of the body, the training which it should have done on earth: but in the end it will get to where it truly wants to be. There is no power in this world or the next that can keep a soul from God if God is what it really desires.

But if, seeing God, the soul rejects Him in hatred and horror, then there is nothing more that God can do for it. God, who has toiled to win it for Himself, and borne for its sake to know death, and suffer the shame of sin, and set His feet in Hell, will nevertheless, if it insists, give it what it desires. The people who think that if God were truly nice and kind He would let us have everything we fancy, are really demanding that He should give us freehold of Hell. And if that is our deliberate and final choice, if with our whole selves we are determined to have nothing but self, He will, in the end, say, "Take it." He cannot, against our own will, force us into Heaven, in the spirit of "I've brought you out to enjoy yourself and you gotter enjoy yourself". Heaven would then be a greater agony than Hell—or rather, Hell *is* Heaven as seen by those who reject it: just as the agonies of the jealous *are* love, seen through the distorting illusion.

IPD 66

. . . it is of the essence of heaven and hell that one must abide for ever with that which one has chosen.

FPD 62

The widespread disinclination to-day to take Hell and Heaven seriously results, very largely, from a refusal to take this world seriously. If we are materialists, we look upon man's life as an event so trifling compared to the cosmic process that our acts and decisions have no importance beyond the little space-time frame in which we find ourselves. If we take what is often vaguely called "a more spiritual attitude to life", we find that we are postulating some large and lazy cosmic benevolence which ensures that, no matter how we behave, it will all somehow or other come out right in the long run. But Christianity says, "No. What you do and what you are matters, and matters intensely. It matters now and it matters eternally; it matters to you, and it matters so much to God that it was for Him literally a matter of life and death."

IPD 100

... there seems to be a kind of conspiracy, especially among middle-aged writers of vaguely liberal tendency, to forget, or to conceal, where the doctrine of Hell comes from. One finds frequent references to "the cruel and abominable mediaeval doctrine of hell", or "the childish and grotesque mediaeval imagery of physical fire and worms". . . .

But the case is quite otherwise; let us face the facts. The doctrine of Hell is not "mediaeval": it is Christ's. It is not a device of "mediaeval priestcraft" for frightening people into giving money to the Church: It is Christ's deliberate judgment on sin. The imagery of the undying worm and the unquenchable fire derives, not from "mediaeval superstition", but originally from the Prophet Isaiah, and it was Christ who emphatically used it. If we are Christians, very well; we dare not not take the doctrine of Hell seriously, for we have it from Him whom we acknowledge as God and Truth incarnate. If we say that Christ was a great and good man, and that, ignoring His divine claims, we should yet stick to His teaching—very well; *that* is what Christ taught. It confronts us in the oldest and least "edited" of the Gospels: it is explicit in many of the most familiar parables and implicit in many more: it bulks far larger in the teaching than one realises, until one reads the Evangelists through instead of merely picking out the most comfortable texts: one cannot get rid of it without tearing the New Testament to tatters. We cannot repudiate Hell without altogether repudiating Christ.

IPD 44

I ought perhaps to say one word about the question which still sometimes bothers people, namely whether the Church officially teaches that the pains of Hell and the joys of Heaven are physical or "only" spiritual. On this side of the Resurrection, the souls have no bodies: consequently the question has no meaning—or at most resolves itself into the rather academical one, discussed with some ingenuity by St Augustine, whether and how a spiritual being can suffer pain from a physical fire. After the Resurrection, there will be a body; but it will be, as St. Paul says, "a spiritual body", and since we do not know at all what it will be like, we cannot tell how it may be able to suffer or rejoice. The danger of saying explicitly, as some theologians have always said, that the pains and joys of spirits are wholly spiritual is that the sort of person who reads *The Freethinker* is then moved to say: "Oh, merely figurative"—as though nothing were really real except the pleasure of sun-bathing and the pains of toothache. What is meant by the stress some-times laid upon the physical aspect of both pain and joy is that it is real, and that it involves the whole personality.

IPD 99

. . . we cannot but be sharply struck by the fact that two of our favourite catch-words have absolutely no mean-ing in Heaven: there is no *equality* and there is no *prog-ress*. Perhaps I should modify that a little: there is equality in the sense that all the souls alike are as full of bliss as they are capable of being: but between soul and soul there is no formal equality at all. The pint-pot and the quart-pot are *equally full:* but there is no pretence that a pint and a quart are the same thing; neither does the pint-pot ever dream of saying to the quart-pot, "I'm as good as you are"—still less of saying "It isn't fair that you should hold more than I." The old sin of Envy, which unleashed the She-Wolf of Avarice from Hell, is utterly extinguished in Heaven. And there is no progress at all in the sense of "bettering one's self" or "getting even with other people".

IPD 57

This tension between joy and the opposite of joy is, once again, something that is viewed with a certain distrust by an age committed to the pursuit of happiness. It can be readily pigeonholed as lack of adjustment or, in severe cases, as a psychosis. In very severe cases it may indeed be a psychosis. But we must not disguise from ourselves that happiness is a gift of the heathen gods, whereas joy is a Christian duty. It was, I think, L. P. Jacks who pointed out that the word "happiness" does not occur in the Gospels; the world "joy", on the other hand, occurs frequently—and so does the name and image of Hell. The command is to rejoice: not to display a placid contentment or a stoic fortitude. "Call no man happy until he is dead", said the Greek philosopher; and happiness, whether applied to a man's fortunes or his disposition, is the assessment of something extended in time along his whole career. But joy (except for those saints who live continually in the presence of God) is of its nature brief and almost instantaneous—it is an apprehension of the eternal moment. And, as such, it is the great invading adversary that can break open the gates of Hell.

PSPS 84

Language

$\mathcal{T}$EAR OFF the disguise of the Jacobean Idiom, go back to the homely and vigorous Greek of Mark or John, translate it into its current English counterpart, and there every man may see his own face.   *MBTK* 23

Reasoning is but words—God's act is the living truth.
                                    EC 149

Earth and water and air—but the beginning and the end-
    ing is fire,
Light in the first day, fire in the last day, at the coming of
    the Word,
And Our Lord the Spirit descending in light and in fire.
                                    EC 27

The education that we have so far succeeded in giving to the bulk of our citizens has produced a generation of mental slatterns. They are literate in the merely formal sense—that is, they are capable of putting the symbols C, A, T together to produce the word CAT. But they are not literate in the sense of deriving from those letters any clear mental concept of the animal. Literacy in the formal sense is dangerous, since it lays the mind open to receive any mischievous nonsense about cats that an irresponsible writer may choose to print—nonsense which could never have entered the heads of plain illiterates who were familiar with an actual cat, even if unable to spell its name. And particularly in the matter of Christian doctrine, a great part of the nation subsists in an ignorance more barbarous than that of the dark ages, owing to this slatternly habit of illiterate reading. Words are understood in a wholly mistaken sense, statements of fact and opinion are misread and distorted in repetition, arguments founded in misapprehension are accepted without examination, expressions of individual preference are construed as oecumenical doctrine, disciplinary regulations founded on consent are confused with claims to interpret universal law, and vice versa; with the result that the logical and historical structure of Christian philosophy is transformed in the popular mind to a confused jumble of mythological and pathological absurdity.

MM xi

Moreover, whether we are dealing with simile or metaphor, it has to be remembered that every image is true and helpful only at its relevant point. God is, in a manner, light: but He is not a succession of wave-lengths in the prime matter. My love is like a red, red rose: but it is not advisable to mulch her with manure. The common sense of mankind can usually be trusted to disentangle the relevant from the irrelevant—but not always. The great dispute that was fought out at Nicaea turned upon the relevant point of a metaphor. That the Divine Son was begotten of the Divine Father was common ground; the Arians, a literal-minded set of people, argued that He must therefore be subsequent to Him, like a bodily procreation. The Orthodox, more sensitively aware of the trap concealed in metaphor, rejected the temptation to enclose God in space-time, holding stubbornly to the paradox of the Son's co-eternity. Indeed, nearly all heresies arise from the pressing of a metaphor beyond the point where the image ceases to be relevant.

PSPS 284

The average modern man is not trained either to understand the grammatical structure of language, or to express his meaning with precision, or to detect fallacies in argument. (Children are indeed encouraged to "express themselves"—but that is a very different matter, and "themselves" is about all that they express.)

FPD 86

Women

*T*HE QUESTION of "sex-equality" is, like all questions affecting human relationships, delicate and complicated. It cannot be settled by loud slogans or hard-and-fast assertions like "a woman is as good as a man"—or "woman's place is in the home"—or "women ought not to take men's jobs." The minute one makes such assertions one finds one has to qualify them. "A woman is as good as a man" is as meaningless as to say, "A Kaffir is as good as a Frenchman" or "a poet is as good as an engineer" or "an elephant is as good as a racehorse"—it means nothing whatever until you add: "at doing what?"

UO 129

What is repugnant to every human being is to be reckoned always as a member of a class and not as an individual person.

UO 130

It is ridiculous to take on a man's job just in order to be able to say that "a woman has done it—yah!" The only decent reason for tackling a job is that it is *your* job, and *you* want to do it.

UO 133

... the average woman of intelligence is fairly ready to believe in the value of a personal relationship, but the idea of a peculiar *mana* attached to femaleness as such, deriving as it does from primitive fertility-cults and nature-magic, is likely to strike her as either nonsensical or repellent.

Purg. 38

. . . there is perhaps only one human being in a thousand who is passionately interested in his job for the job's sake. The difference is that if that one person in a thousand is a man, we say, simply, that he is passionately keen on his job; if she is a woman, we say she is a freak.

UO 135

I think I have never heard a sermon preached on the story of Martha and Mary that did not attempt, somehow, somewhere, to explain away its text. Mary's of course was the better part—the Lord said so, and we must not precisely contradict Him. But we will be careful not to despise Martha. No doubt, He approved of her too. We could not get on without her, and indeed (having paid lip-service to God's opinion) we must admit that we greatly prefer her. For Martha was doing a really feminine job, whereas Mary was just behaving like any other disciple, male or female; and that is a hard pill to swallow.

UO 148

Perhaps it is no wonder that the women were first at the Cradle and last at the Cross. They had never known a man like this Man—there never has been such another. A prophet and teacher who never nagged at them, never flattered or coaxed or patronised; who never made arch jokes about them, never treated them either as "The women, God help us!" or "The ladies, God bless them!"; who rebuked without querulousness and praised without condescension; who took their questions and arguments seriously; who never mapped out their sphere for them, never urged them to be feminine or jeered at them for being female; who had no axe to grind and no uneasy male dignity to defend; who took them as he found them and was completely unself-conscious. There is no act, no sermon, no parable in the whole Gospel that borrows its pungency from female perversity; nobody could guess from the words and deeds of Jesus that there was anything "funny" about woman's nature.

UO 148

Work

NOT WITH the lips alone,
But with the hand and with the cunning brain
Men worship the eternal Architect.
So, when the mouth is dumb, the work shall speak
And save the workman.

ZH 34

"The hatred of work must be one of the most depressing consequences of the Fall."

ZH 13

When a story is great enough, any honest craftsman may succeed in producing something not altogether unworthy, because the greatness is in the story, and does not need to borrow anything from the craftsman; it is enough that he should faithfully serve the work.

MBTK 36-37

We may perhaps go so far as to assert that the Trinitarian structure of activity is mysterious to us just because it is universal—rather as the four-dimensional structure of space-time is mysterious because we cannot get outside it to look at it. The mathematician can, however, to some extent perform the intellectual feat of observing space-time from without, and we may similarly call upon the creative artist to extricate himself from his own activity far enough to examine and describe its three-fold structure.

For the purpose of this examination I shall use the mind of the creative writer, both because I am more familiar with its workings than with those of other creative artists, and because I shall thus save the confusion of a great many clauses beginning with "and" and "or". But, *mutatis mutandis,* what is true of the writer is true also of the painter, the musician and all workers of creative imagination in whatever form. "The writer" is of course understood to be the ideal writer, considered when engaged in an act of artistic creation, just as, in considering the "father," we always intend the ideal parent, considered while exercising the functions of parenthood and in no other activity. It is not to be imagined that any human writer ever works with ideal perfection; in the tenth chapter of this book I shall try to point out what happens when the writer's trinity fails too conspicuously to conform to the law of its own nature —for here, as always, there is a judgment for behavior that runs counter to the law.

Since this chapter—and indeed this whole book—is an expansion of the concluding speech of St. Michael in my play *The Zeal of Thy House,* it will perhaps be convenient to quote that speech here:

"For every work [or act] of creation is threefold, an earthly trinity to match the heavenly.

"First, [not in time, but merely in order of enumeration] there is the Creative Idea, passionless, timeless, beholding the whole work complete at once, the end in the beginning: and this is the image of the Father.

"Second, there is the Creative Energy [or Activity] begotten of that idea, working in time from the beginning to the end, with sweat and passion, being incarnate in the bonds of matter: and this is the image of the Word.

"Third, there is the Creative Power, the meaning of the work and its response in the lively soul: and this is the image of the indwelling Spirit.

"And these three are one, each equally in itself the whole work, whereof none can exist without other: and this is the image of the Trinity."

Of these clauses, the one which gives the most trouble to the hearer is that dealing with the Creative Idea. (The word is here used, not in the philosopher's sense, in which the "Idea" tends to be equated with the "Word", but quite simply in the sense intended by the writer when he says: "I have an idea for a book.") The ordinary man is apt to say: "I thought you began by collecting material and working out the plot." The confusion here is not merely over the words "first" and "begin". In fact the "Idea"—or rather the writer's realization of his own idea—does precede any mental or physical work upon the materials or on the course of the story within a time-series. But apart from this, the very formulation of the Idea in the writer's mind is not the Idea itself, but its self-awareness in the Energy. Everything that is conscious, everything that has to do with process, belongs to the working of the Energy or Activity or "Word". The Idea, that is, cannot be said to precede the Energy in time, because (so far as that act of creation is concerned) it is the Energy that creates the time process. This is the analogy of the theological expression that "the Word was in the beginning with God" and was "eternally begotten of the Father". If, that is, the act has a beginning in time at all, it is because of the presence of the Energy or Activity. The writer cannot even be conscious of his Idea except by the working of the Energy which formulates it to himself.

That being so, how can we know that the Idea itself has any real existence apart from the Energy? Very strangely; by the fact that the Energy itself is conscious of referring all its acts to an existing and complete whole. In theological terms, the Son does the will of the Father. Quite simply, every choice of an episode, or a phrase, or a word is made to conform to a pattern of the entire book, which is revealed by that choice as already existing. This truth, which is difficult to convey in explanation, is quite clear and obvious in experience. It manifests itself plainly enough when the writer says or thinks: "That is, or is not, the right phrase"—meaning that it is a phrase which does or does not correspond to the reality of the Idea.

Further, although the book—that is, the activity of writing the book—is a process in space and time, it is known to the writer as *also* a complete and timeless whole, "the end in the beginning," and this knowledge of it is with him always, while writing it and after it is finished, just as it was at the beginning. It is not changed or affected by the toils and troubles of composition, nor is the writer aware of his book as merely a succession of words and situations. The Idea of the book is a thing-in-itself quite apart from its awareness or its manifestation in Energy, though it still remains true that it cannot be known as a thing-in-itself except as the Energy reveals it. The Idea is thus timeless and without parts or passions, though it is never seen, either by writer or reader, except in terms of time, parts and passion.

The Energy itself is an easier concept to grasp, because it is the thing of which the writer is conscious and which the reader can see when it is manifest in material form. It is dynamic—the sum and process of all the activity which brings the book into temporal and spatial existence. "All things are made by it, and without it nothing is made that has been made." To it belongs everything that can be included under the word "passion"—feeling, thought, toil, trouble, difficulty, choice, triumph— all the accidents which attend a manifestation in time. It is the Energy that is the creator in the sense in which the common man understands the word, because it brings about an expression in temporal form of the eternal and immutable Idea. It is, for the writer, what he means by "the writing of the book", and it includes, though it is not confined to, the manifestation of the book in material form. We shall have more to say about it in the following chapters: for the moment, the thing I am anxious to establish is that it is something distinct from the Idea itself, though it is the only thing that can make the Idea known to itself or to others, and yet is (in the ideal creative act which we are considering) essentially identical with the Idea—"consubstantial with the Father".

The Creative Power is the third "Person" of the writer's trinity. It is not the same thing as the Energy (which for greater clearness I ought perhaps to have called "the Activity"), though it proceeds from the Idea and the Energy together. It is the thing which flows back to the writer from his own activity and makes him, as it were, the reader of his own book. It is also, of course, the means by which the Activity is communicated to other readers and which produces a corresponding response in them. In fact, from the reader's point of view, it *is* the book. By it, they perceive the book, both as a process in time and as an eternal whole, and react to it dynamically. It is at this point we begin to understand what St. Hilary means in saying of the Trinity: "Eternity is in the Father, form in the Image and use in the Gift".

Lastly: "These three are one, each equally in itself the whole work, whereof none can exist without other." If you were to ask a writer which is "the real book"— his Idea of it, his Activity in writing it, or its return to himself in Power, he would be at a loss to tell you, because these things are essentially inseparable. Each of them is the complete book separately; yet in the complete book all of them exist together. He can, by an act of the intellect, "distinguish the persons" but he cannot by any means "divide the substance". How could he? He cannot know the Idea, except by the Power interpreting his own Activity to him; he knows the Activity only as it reveals the Idea in Power; he knows the Power only as the reve-

lation of the Idea in the Activity. All he can say is that
these three are equally and eternally present in his own
act of creation, and at every moment of it, whether or
not the act ever becomes manifest in the form of a written and printed book. These things are not confined to
the material manifestation: they exist in—they *are*—the
creative mind itself.

MM 36-41

The Church's approach to an intelligent carpenter is
usually confined to exhorting him not to be drunk and
disorderly in his leisure hours, and to come to church on
Sundays. What the Church *should* be telling him is this:
that the very first demand that his religion makes upon
him is that he should make good tables. Church by all
means, and decent forms of amusement, certainly—but
what use is all that if in the very centre of his life and
occupation he is insulting God with bad carpentry? No
crooked table-legs or ill-fitting drawers ever, I dare
swear, came out of the carpenter's shop at Nazareth.
Nor, if they did, could anyone believe that they were
made by the same hand that made heaven and earth. No
piety in the worker will compensate for work that is not
true to itself; for any work that is untrue to its own technique is a living lie. Yet in her own buildings, in her own
ecclesiastical art and music, in her hymns and prayers,
in her sermons and in her little books of devotion,
the Church will tolerate, or permit a pious intention to
excuse, work so ugly, so pretentious, so tawdry and
twaddling, so insincere and insipid, so *bad* as to shock
and horrify any decent craftsman. And why? Simply
because she has lost all sense of the fact that the living
and eternal truth is expressed in work only so far as that
work is true in itself, to itself, to the standards of its
own technique. She has forgotten that the secular voca-

tion is sacred. Forgotten that a building must be good architecture before it can be a good church; that a painting must be well painted before it can be a good sacred picture; that work must be good work before it can call itself God's work.

CC 56-57

[On Usury] ... there are only two sources of real wealth: Nature and Art—or, as we should put it, Natural Resources and the Labour of Man. The buying and selling of Money as though it were a commodity creates only a spurious wealth, and results in injury to the earth (Nature) and the exploitation of labour (Art). The attitude to men and things which this implies is a kind of blasphemy; since Art derives from Nature, as Nature derives from God, so that contempt of them is contempt of Him.

Hell 140

If you want to realise how deeply the economic standard of value has bitten into the public mind, you should witness the desperate attempts of the scholar or artist to explain to someone who has given him an order for work that he is not primarily concerned with the money, but with getting the work properly done.

BH 103

The habit of thinking about work as something one does to make money is so ingrained in us that we can scarcely imagine what a revolutionary change it would be to think about it instead in terms of the work done.

CC 51

The official Church wastes time and energy, and, moreover, commits sacrilege, in demanding that secular workers should neglect their proper vocation in order to do
Christian work—by which she means ecclesiastical work.
The only Christian work is good work well done.

CC 57-58

The Lost Tools
of Learning

$\mathcal{T}$HAT I, whose experience of teaching is extremely limited, and whose life of recent years has been almost wholly out of touch with educational circles, should presume to discuss education is a matter, surely, that calls for no apology. It is a kind of behaviour to which the present climate of opinion is wholly favourable. Bishops air their opinions about economics; biologists, about metaphysics; celibates, about matrimony; inorganic chemists about theology; the most irrelevant people are appointed to highly-technical ministries; and plain, blunt men write to the papers to say that Epstein and Picasso do not know how to draw. Up to a certain point, and provided that the criticisms are made with a reasonable modesty, these activities are commendable. Too much specialisation is not a good thing. There is also one excellent reason why the veriest amateur may feel entitled to have an opinion about education. For if we are not all professional teachers, we have all, at some time or other, been taught. Even if we learnt nothing—perhaps in particular if we learnt nothing—our contribution to the discussion may have a potential value.

Without apology, then, I will begin. But since much that I have to say is highly controversial, it will be pleasant to start with a proposition with which, I feel confident, all teachers will cordially agree; and that is, that they all work much too hard and have far too many things to do. One has only to look at any school or examination syllabus to see that it is cluttered up with a great variety of exhausting subjects which they are called upon to teach, and the teaching of which sadly interferes with what every thoughtful mind will allow to be their proper duties, such as distributing milk, supervising meals, taking cloak-room duty, weighing and measuring pupils, keeping their eyes open for incipient mumps, measles and chicken-pox, making out lists, escorting parties round the Victoria and Albert Museum, filling up forms, interviewing parents, and devising end-of-term reports which shall combine a deep veneration for truth with a tender respect for the feelings of all concerned.

Upon these really important duties I will not enlarge. I propose only to deal with the subject of teaching, properly so-called. I want to inquire whether, amid all the multitudinous subjects which figure in the syllabuses, we are really teaching the right things in the right way; and whether, by teaching fewer things, differently, we might not succeed in "shedding the load" (as the fashionable phrase goes) and, at the same time, producing a better result.

This prospect need arouse neither hope nor alarm. It is in the highest degree improbable that the reforms I propose will ever be carried into effect. Neither the parents, nor the training colleges, nor the examination boards, nor the boards of governors, nor the Ministry of Education would countenance them for a moment. For they amount to this: that if we are to produce a society of educated people, fitted to preserve their intellectual freedom amid the complex pressures of our modern society, we must turn back the wheel of progress some four or five hundred years, to the point at which education began to lose sight of its true object, towards the end of the Middle Ages.

Before you dismiss me with the appropriate phrase— reactionary, romantic, mediaevalist, *laudator temporis acti,* or whatever tag comes first to hand—I will ask you to consider one or two miscellaneous questions that hang about at the back, perhaps, of all our minds, and occasionally pop out to worry us.

When we think about the remarkably early age at which the young men went up to the University in, let us say, Tudor times, and thereafter were held fit to assume responsibility for the conduct of their own affairs, are we altogether comfortable about that artificial prolongation of intellectual childhood and adolescence into the years of physical maturity which is so marked in our own day? To postpone the acceptance of responsibility to a late date brings with it a number of psychological complications which, while they may interest the psychiatrist, are scarcely beneficial either to the individual or to society. The stock argument in favour of postponing the school leaving-age and prolonging the period of education generally is that there is now so much more to learn than there was in the Middle Ages. This is partly true, but not wholly. The modern boy and girl are certainly taught more subjects—but does that always mean that they are actually more learned and know more? That is the very point which we are going to consider.

Has it ever struck you as odd, or unfortunate, that to-day, when the proportion of literacy throughout Western Europe is higher than it has ever been, people should have become susceptible to the influence of advertisement and mass-propaganda to an extent hitherto unheard-of and unimagined? Do you put this down to the mere mechanical fact that the press and the radio and so on have made propaganda much easier to distribute over a wide area? Or do you sometimes have an uneasy suspicion that the product of modern educational methods is less good than he or she might be at disentangling fact from opinion and the proven from the plausible?

Have you ever, in listening to a debate among adult and presumably responsible people, been fretted by the extraordinary inability of the average debater to speak to the question, or to meet and refute the arguments of speakers on the other side? Or have you ever pondered upon the extremely high incidence of irrelevant matter which crops up at committee-meetings, and upon the very great rarity of persons capable of acting as chairmen of committees? And when you think of this, and think that most of our public affairs are settled by debates and committees, have you ever felt a certain sinking of the heart?

Have you ever followed a discussion in the newspapers or elsewhere and noticed how frequently writers fail to define the terms they use? Or how often, if one man does define his terms, another will assume in his reply that he was using the terms in precisely the opposite sense to that in which he has already defined them?

Have you ever been faintly troubled by the amount of slipshod syntax going about? And if so, are you troubled because it is inelegant or because it may lead to dangerous misunderstanding?

Do you ever find that young people, when they have left school, not only forget most of what they have learnt (that is only to be expected) but forget also, or betray that they have never really known, how to tackle a new subject for themselves? Are you often bothered by coming across grown-up men and women who seem unable to distinguish between a book that is sound, scholarly and properly documented, and one that is to any trained eye, very conspicuously none of these things? Or who cannot handle a library catalogue? Or who, when faced with a book of reference, betray a curious inability to extract from it the passages relevant to the particular question which interests them?

Do you often come across people for whom, all their lives, a "subject" remains a "subject," divided by watertight bulkheads from all other "subjects," so that they experience very great difficulty in making an immediate mental connection between, let us say, algebra and detective fiction, sewage disposal and the price of salmon, cellulose and the distribution of rainfall—or, more generally, between such spheres of knowledge as philosophy and economics, or chemistry and art?

Are you occasionally perturbed by the things written by adult men and women for adult men and women to read? Here, for instance, is a quotation from an evening paper. It refers to the visit of an Indian girl to this country:—

> Miss Bhosle has a perfect command of English ("Oh, gosh," she said once), and a marked enthusiasm for London.

Well, we may all talk nonsense in a moment of inattention. It is more alarming when we find a well-known biologist writing in a weekly paper to the effect that: "It is an argument against the existence of a Creator" (I think he put it more strongly; but since I have, most unfortunately, mislaid the reference, I will put his claim at its lowest)—"an argument against the existence of a Creator that the same kind of variations which are produced by natural selection can be produced at will by stock-breeders." One might feel tempted to say that it is rather an argument *for* the existence of a Creator. Actually, of course, it is neither: all it proves is that the same material causes (re-combination of the chromosomes by cross-breeding and so forth) are sufficient to account for all observed variations—just as the various combinations of the same 13 semitones are materially sufficient to account for Beethoven's *Moonlight Sonata* and the noise the cat makes by walking on the keys. But the cat's performance neither proves nor disproves the existence of Beethoven; and all that is proved by the biologist's argument is that he was unable to distinguish between a material and a final cause.

Here is a sentence from no less academic a source than a front-page article in the *Times Literary Supplement:*—

> The Frenchman, Alfred Epinas, pointed out that certain species (*e.g.,* ants and wasps) can only face the horrors of life and death in association.

I do not know what the Frenchman actually did say: what the Englishman says he said is patently meaningless. We cannot know whether life holds any horror for the ant, nor in what sense the isolated wasp which you kill upon the window-pane can be said to "face" or not to "face" the horrors of death. The subject of the article is mass-behaviour in *man;* and the human motives have been unobtrusively transferred from the main proposition to the supporting instance. Thus the argument, in effect, assumes what it sets out to prove—a fact which would become immediately apparent if it were presented in a formal syllogism. This is only a small and haphazard example of a vice which pervades whole books—particularly books written by men of science on metaphysical subjects.

Another quotation from the same issue of the *T.L.S.* comes in fittingly here to wind up this random collection of disquieting thoughts—this time from a review of Sir Richard Livingstone's *Some Tasks for Education:*—

> More than once the reader is reminded of the value of an intensive study of at least one subject, so as to learn "the meaning of knowledge" and what precision and persistence is needed to attain it. Yet there is elsewhere full recognition of the distressing fact that a man may be master in one field and show no better judgment than his neighbour anywhere else; he remembers what he has learnt, but forgets altogether how he learned it.

I would draw your attention particularly to that last sentence, which offers an explanation of what the writer rightly calls the "distressing fact" that the intellectual skills bestowed upon us by our education are not readily transferable to subjects other than those in which we acquired them: "he remembers what he has learnt, but forgets altogether how he learned it."

Is not the great defect of our education to-day—a defect traceable through all the disquieting symptoms of trouble that I have mentioned—that although we often succeed in teaching our pupils "subjects," we fail lamentably on the whole in teaching them how to think? They learn everything, except the art of learning. It is as though we had taught a child, mechanically and by rule of thumb, to play *The Harmonious Blacksmith* upon the piano, but had never taught him the scale or how to read music; so that, having memorised *The Harmonious Blacksmith,* he still had not the faintest notion how to proceed from that to tackle *The Last Rose of Summer.* Why do I say, "As though"? In certain of the arts and crafts we sometimes do precisely this— requiring a child to "express himself" in paint before we teach him how to handle the colours and the brush. There is a school of thought which believes this to be the right way to set about the job. But observe—it is not the way in which a trained craftsman will go about to teach himself a new medium. *He,* having learned by experience the best way to economise labour and take the thing by the right end, will start off by doodling about on an odd piece of material, in order to "give himself the feel of the tool."

Let us now look at the mediaeval scheme of education —the syllabus of the Schools. It does not matter, for the moment, whether it was devised for small children or for older students; or how long people were supposed to take over it. What matters is the light it throws upon what the men of the Middle Ages supposed to be the object and the right order of the educative process.

The syllabus was divided into two parts: the Trivium and Quadrivium. The second part—the Quadrivium— consisted of "subjects," and need not for the moment concern us. The interesting thing for us is the composition of the Trivium, which preceded the Quadrivium and

was the preliminary discipline for it. It consisted of three
parts: Grammar, Dialectic, and Rhetoric, in that order.

Now the first thing we notice is that two at any rate
of these "subjects" are not what we should call "subjects" at all: they are only methods of dealing with
subjects. Grammar, indeed, is a "subject" in the sense
that it does mean definitely learning a language—at that
period it meant learning Latin. But language itself is
simply the medium in which thought is expressed. The
whole of the Trivium was, in fact, intended to teach the
pupil the proper use of the tools of learning, before he
began to apply them to "subjects" at all. First, he learned
a language; not just how to order a meal in a foreign language, but the structure of language—*a* language, and
hence of language itself—what it was, how it was put
together and how it worked. Secondly, he learned how to
use language: how to define his terms and make accurate
statements; how to construct an argument and how to
detect fallacies in argument (his own arguments and
other people's). Dialectic, that is to say, embraced Logic
and Disputation. Thirdly, he learned to express himself
in language; how to say what he had to say elegantly and
persuasively. At this point, any tendency to express himself windily or to use his eloquence so as to make the
worse appear the better reason would, no doubt, be re-
strained by his previous teaching in Dialectic. If not, his
teacher and his fellow-pupils, trained along the same
lines, would be quick to point out where he was wrong;
for it was they whom he had to seek to persuade. At the
end of his course, he was required to compose a thesis
upon some theme set by his masters or chosen by himself, and afterwards to defend his thesis against the criticism of the faculty. By this time he would have learned
—or woe betide him—not merely to write an essay on
paper, but to speak audibly and intelligibly from a platform, and to use his wits quickly when heckled. The

heckling, moreover, would not consist solely of offensive personalities or of irrelevant queries about what Julius Caesar said in 55 B.C.—though no doubt mediaeval dialectic was enlivened in practice by plenty of such primitive repartee. But there would also be questions, cogent and shrewd, from those who had already run the gauntlet of debate, or were making ready to run it.

It is, of course, quite true that bits and pieces of the mediaeval tradition still linger, or have been revived, in the ordinary school syllabus of to-day. Some knowledge of grammar is still required when learning a foreign language—perhaps I should say, "is again required"; for during my own lifetime we passed through a phase when the teaching of declensions and conjugations was considered rather reprehensible, and it was considered better to pick these things up as we went along. School debating societies flourish; essays are written; the necessity for "self-expression" is stressed, and perhaps even over-stressed. But these activities are cultivated more or less in detachment, as belonging to the special subjects in which they are pigeon-holed rather than as forming one coherent scheme of mental training to which all "subjects" stand in a subordinate relation. "Grammar" belongs especially to the "subject" of foreign languages, and essay-writing to the "subject" called "English"; while Dialectic has become almost entirely divorced from the rest of the curriculum, and is frequently practised unsystematically and out of school-hours as a separate exercise, only very loosely related to the main business of learning. Taken by and large, the great difference of emphasis between the two conceptions holds good: modern education concentrates on *teaching subjects,* leaving the method of thinking, arguing and expressing one's conclusions to be picked up by the scholar as he goes along; mediaeval education concentrated on first *forging and learning to handle the tools of learning,* using whatever subject came handy as a piece of material on which to doodle until the use of the tool became second nature.

"Subjects" of some kind there must be, of course. One cannot learn the use of a tool by merely waving it in the air; neither can one learn the theory of grammar without learning an actual language, or learn to argue and orate without speaking about something in particular. The debating subjects of the Middle Ages were drawn largely from Theology, or from the Ethics and History of Antiquity. Often, indeed, they became stereotyped, especially towards the end of the period, and the far-fetched and wire-drawn absurdities of scholastic argument fretted Milton and provide food for merriment even to this day. Whether they were in themselves any more hackneyed and trivial than the usual subjects set nowadays for "essay-writing" I should not like to say: we may ourselves grow a little weary of 'A Day in my Holidays," "What I should like to Do when I Leave School," and all the rest of it. But most of the merriment is misplaced, because the aim and object of the debating thesis has by now been lost sight of. A glib speaker in the Brains Trust once entertained his audience (and reduced the late Charles Williams to helpless rage) by asserting that in the Middle Ages it was a matter of faith to know how many archangels could dance on the point of a needle. I need not say, I hope, that it never was a "matter of faith"; it was simply a debating exercise, whose set subject was the nature of angelic substance: were angels material, and if so, did they occupy space? The answer usually adjudged correct is, I believe, that angels are pure intelligences; not material, but limited, so that they may have location in space but not extension. An analogy might be drawn from human thought, which is similarly non-material and similarly limited. Thus, if your thought is concentrated upon one thing—say, the point of a needle—it is located there in the sense that it is not elsewhere; but although it is "there," it occupies no space there, and there is nothing to prevent an infinite number of different people's thoughts being concentrated upon the same needle-point at the same time. The proper *subject* of the argument is thus seen to be the distinction between location and extension in space; the *matter* on which the argument is exercised happens to be the nature of angels (although, as we have seen, it might equally well have something else); the practical lesson to be drawn from the argument is not to use words like "there" in a loose and unscientific way, without specifying whether you mean "located there" or "occupying space there." Scorn in plenty has been poured out upon the mediaeval passion for hair-splitting: but when we look at the shameless abuse made, in print and on the platform, of controversial expressions with shifting and ambiguous connotations, we may feel it in our hearts to wish that every reader and hearer had been so defensively armoured by his education as to be able to cry: *Distinguo.*

For we let our young men and women go out unarmed, in a day when armour was never so necessary. By teaching them all to read, we have left them at the mercy of the printed word. By the invention of the film and the radio, we have made certain that no aversion to reading shall secure them from the incessant battery of words, words, words. They do not know what the words mean; they do not know how to ward them off or blunt their edge or fling them back; they are a prey to words in their emotions instead of being the masters of them in their intellects. We who were scandalised in 1940 when men were sent to fight armoured tanks with rifles, are not scandalized when young men and women are sent into the world to fight massed propaganda with a smattering of "subjects"; and when whole classes and whole

nations become hypnotised by the arts of the spell-
binder, we have the impudence to be astonished. We
dole out lip-service to the importance of education—
lip-service and, just occasionally, a little grant of money;
we postpone the school leaving-age, and plan to build
bigger and better schools; the teachers slave conscien-
tiously in and out of school-hours, till responsibility becomes a burden and a nightmare; and yet, as I believe,
all this devoted effort is largely frustrated, because we
have lost the tools of learning, and in their absence can
only make a botched and piecemeal job of it.

What, then, are we to do? We cannot go back to the
Middle Ages. That is a cry to which we have become
accustomed. We cannot go back—or can we? *Distinguo.*
I should like every term in that proposition defined.
Does "Go back" mean a retrogression in time, or the
revision of an error? The first is clearly impossible *per
se*; the second is a thing which wise men do every day.
"Cannot"—does this mean that our behaviour is determined by some irreversible cosmic mechanism, or
merely that such an action would be very difficult in
view of the opposition it would provoke? "The Middle
Ages"—obviously the 20th century is not and cannot
be the 14th; but if "Middle Ages" is, in this context,
simply a picturesque phrase denoting a particular educational theory, there seems to be no *a priori* reason why
we should not "go back" to it—with modifications—as
we have already "gone back," with modifications, to, let
us say, the idea of playing Shakespeare's plays as he
wrote them, and not in the "modernised" versions of
Cibber and Garrick, which once seemed to be the latest
thing in theatrical progress.

Let us amuse ourselves by imagining that such pro-
gressive retrogression is possible. Let us make a clean
sweep of all educational authorities, and furnish ourselves with a nice little school of boys and girls whom

we may experimentally equip for the intellectual con-
flict along lines chosen by ourselves. We will endow
them with exceptionally docile parents; we will staff
our school with teachers who are themselves perfectly
familiar with the aims and methods of the Trivium; we
will have our buildings and staff large enough to allow
our classes to be small enough for adequate handling;
and we will postulate a Board of Examiners willing and
qualified to test the products we turn out. Thus prepared,
we will attempt to sketch out a syllabus—a modern
Trivium "with modifications"; and we will see where
we get to.

But first: what age shall the children be? Well, if
one is to educate them on novel lines, it will be better
that they should have nothing to unlearn; besides, one
cannot begin a good thing too early, and the Trivium
is by its nature not learning, but a preparation for
learning. We will, therefore, "catch 'em young," requiring only of our pupils that they shall be able to read,
write and cipher.

My views about child-psychology are, I admit, neither
orthodox nor enlightened. Looking back upon myself
(since I am the child I know best and the only child I
can pretend to know from inside) I recognise in myself
three stages of development. These, in a rough-and-
ready fashion, I will call the Poll-parrot, the Pert, and
the Poetic—the latter coinciding, approximately, with
the onset of puberty. The Poll-parrot stage is the one
in which learning by heart is easy and, on the whole,
pleasurable; whereas reasoning is difficult and, on the
whole, little relished. At this age, one readily memorises
the shapes and appearances of things; one likes to recite
the number-plates of cars; one rejoices in the chanting
of rhymes and the rumble and thunder of unintelligible
polysyllables; one enjoys the mere accumulation of
things. The Pert Age, which follows upon this (and,

naturally, overlaps it to some extent) is only too familiar
to all who have to do with children: it is characterised
by contradicting, answering-back, liking to "catch
people out" (especially one's elders) and in the pro-
pounding of conundrums (especially the kind with a
nasty verbal catch in them). Its nuisance-value is extremely high. It usually sets in about the Lower Fourth.
The Poetic Age is popularly known as the "difficult"
age. It is self-centred; it yearns to express itself; it rather
specialises in being misunderstood; it is restless and tries
to achieve independence; and, with good luck and good
guidance, it should show the beginnings of creativeness,
a reaching-out towards a synthesis of what it already
knows, and a deliberate eagerness to know and do some
one thing in preference to all others. Now it seems to me
that the lay-out of the Trivium adapts itself with a
singular appropriateness to these three ages: Grammar
to the Poll-parrot, Dialectic to the Pert, and Rhetoric
to the Poetic Age.

Let us begin, then, with Grammar. This, in practice,
means the grammar of some language in particular; and
it must be an inflected language. The grammatical structure of an uninflected language is far too analytical to
be tackled by any one without previous practice in Dialectic. Moreover, the inflected languages interpret the
uninflected, whereas the uninflected are of little use in
interpreting the inflected. I will say at once, quite firmly,
that the best grounding for education is the Latin grammar. I say this, not because Latin is traditional and
mediaeval, but simply because even a rudimentary
knowledge of Latin cuts down the labour and pains of
learning almost any other subject by at least fifty per
cent. It is the key to the vocabulary and structure of
all the Romance languages and to the structure of all
the Teutonic languages, as well as to the technical vocabulary of all the sciences and to the literature of the

entire Mediterranean civilisation, together with all its
historical documents. Those whose pedantic preference
for a living language persuades them to deprive their
pupils of all these advantages might substitute Russian,
whose grammar is still more primitive. (The verb is
complicated by a number of "aspects"—and I rather
fancy that it enjoys three complete voices and a couple
of extra aorists—but I may be thinking of Basque or
Sanskrit.) Russian is, of course, helpful with the other
Slav dialects. There is something also to be said for
Classical Greek. But my own choice is Latin. Having
thus pleased the Classicists among you, I will proceed
to horrify them by adding that I do not think it either
wise or necessary to cramp the ordinary pupil upon the
Procrustean bed of the Augustan age, with its highly
elaborate and artificial verse-forms and oratory. The
post-classical and mediaeval Latin, which was a living
language down to the end of the Renaissance, is easier
and in some ways livelier, both in syntax and rhythm;
and a study of it helps to dispel the widespread notion
that learning and literature came to a full-stop when
Christ was born and only woke up again at the Dissolu-
tion of the Monasteries.

However, I am running ahead too fast. We are still
in the grammatical stage. Latin should be begun as
early as possible—at a time when inflected speech seems
no more astonishing than any other phenomenon in an
astonishing world; and when the chanting of "amo,
amas, amat" is as ritually agreeable to the feelings as the
chanting of "eeny, meeny, miney, mo."

During this age we must, of course, exercise the mind
on other things besides Latin grammar. Observation and
memory are the faculties most lively at this period; and
if we are to learn a contemporary foreign language we
should begin now, before the facial and mental muscles
become rebellious to strange intonations. Spoken French

or German can be practised alongside the grammatical discipline of the Latin.

In *English*, verse and prose can be learned by heart, and the pupil's memory should be stored with stories of every kind—classical myth, European legend, and so forth. I do not think that the Classical stories and masterpieces of ancient literature should be made the vile bodies on which to practise the technics of Grammar —that was a fault of mediaeval education which we need not perpetrate. The stories can be enjoyed and remembered in English, and related to their origin at a subsequent stage. Recitation aloud should be practised— individually or in chorus; for we must not forget that we are laying the ground work for Disputation and Rhetoric.

The grammar of *History* should consist, I think, of dates, events, anecdotes and personalities. A set of dates to which one can peg all later historical knowledge is of enormous help later on in establishing the perspective of history. It does not greatly matter *which* dates: those of the Kings of England will do very nicely, provided that they are accompanied by pictures of costume, architecture, and other "every-day things," so that the mere mention of a date calls up a strong visual presentment of the whole period.

Geography will similarly be presented in its factual aspect, with maps, natural features and visual presentment of customs, costumes, flora, fauna and so on; and I believe myself that the discredited and old-fashioned memorizing of a few capital cities, rivers, mountain ranges, etc., does no harm. Stamp-collecting may be encouraged.

Science, in the Poll-parrot period, arranges itself naturally and easily round collections—the identifying and naming of specimens and, in general, the kind of thing that used to be called "natural history," or, still more charmingly, "natural philosophy." To know the names and properties of things is, at this age, a satisfaction in itself; to recognise a devil's coach-horse at sight, and assure one's foolish elders that, in spite of its appearance, it does not sting; to be able to pick out Cassiopeia and the Pleiades, and possibly even to know who Cassiopeia and the Pleiades were; to be aware that a whale is not a fish, and a bat not a bird—all these things give a pleasant sensation of superiority; while to know a ring-snake from an adder or a poisonous from an edible toadstool is a kind of knowledge that has also a practical value.

The grammar of *Mathematics* begins, of course, with the multiplication table, which, if not learnt now, will never be learnt with pleasure; and with the recognition of geometrical shapes and the grouping of numbers. These exercises lead naturally to the doing of simple sums in arithmetic; and if the pupil shows a bent that way, a facility acquired at this stage is all to the good. More complicated mathematical processes may, and perhaps should, be postponed, for reasons which will presently appear.

So far (except, of course, for the Latin) our curriculum contains nothing that departs very far from common practice. The difference will be felt rather in the attitude of the teachers, who must look upon all these activities less as "subjects" in themselves than as a gathering-together of *material* for use in the next part of the Trivium. What that material actually is, is only of secondary importance; but it is as well that anything and everything which can usefully be committed to memory should be memorised at this period, whether it is immediately intelligible or not. The modern tendency is to try and force rational explanations on a child's mind at too early an age. Intelligent questions spontaneously asked, should, of course, receive an immediate and rational answer; but it is a great mistake to suppose that a child cannot readily enjoy and remember things that are beyond its power to analyse—particularly if those things have a strong imaginative appeal (as, for example, *Kubla Khan*), an attractive jingle (like some of the memory-rhymes for Latin genders), or an abundance of rich, resounding polysyllables (like the *Quicunque Vult*).

This reminds me of the Grammar of *Theology*. I shall add it to the curriculum, because Theology is the mistress-science, without which the whole educational structure will necessarily lack its final synthesis. Those who disagree about this will remain content to leave their pupils' education still full of loose ends. This will matter rather less than it might, since by the time that the tools of learning have been forged the student will be able to tackle Theology for himself, and will probably insist upon doing so and making sense of it. Still, it is as well to have this matter also handy and ready for the reason to work upon. At the grammatical age, therefore, we should become acquainted with the story of God and Man in outline—*i.e.*, the Old and New Testament presented as parts of a single narrative of Creation, Rebellion and Redemption—and also with "the Creed, the Lord's Prayer and the Ten Commandments." At this stage, it does not matter nearly so much that these things should be fully understood as that they should be known and remembered. Remember, it is material that we are collecting.

It is difficult to say at what age, precisely, we should pass from the first to the second part of the Trivium. Generally speaking, the answer is: so soon as the pupil shows himself disposed to Pertness and interminable argument (or, as a schoolmaster correspondent of mine more elegantly puts it: "When the capacity for abstract thought begins to manifest itself"). For as, in the first part, the master-faculties are Observation and Memory, so in the second, the master-faculty is the Discursive Reason. In the first, the exercise to which the rest of the material was, as it were, keyed, was the Latin Grammar; in the second the key-exercise will be Formal Logic. It is here that our curriculum shows its first sharp divergence from modern standards. The disrepute into which Formal Logic has fallen is entirely unjustified; and its neglect is the root cause of nearly all those disquieting symptoms which we have noted in the modern intellectual constitution. Logic has been discredited, partly because we have fallen into a habit of supposing that we are conditioned almost entirely by the intuitive and the unconscious. There is no time now to argue whether this is true; I will content myself with observing that to neglect the proper training of the reason is the best possible way to make it true, and to ensure the supremacy of the intuitive, irrational and unconscious elements in our make-up. A secondary cause for the disfavour into which Formal Logic has fallen is the belief that it is entirely based upon universal assumptions that are either unprovable or tautological. This is not true. Not all universal propositions are of this kind. But even if they were, it would make no difference, since every syllogism whose major premise is in the form "All A is B" can be recast in hypothetical form. Logic is the art of arguing correctly: "If A, then B"; the method is not invalidated by the hypothetical character of A. Indeed, the practical utility of Formal Logic to-day lies not so much in the establishment of positive conclusions as in the prompt detection and exposure of invalid inference.

Let us now quickly review our material and see how it is to be related to Dialectic. On the *Language* side, we shall now have our Vocabulary and Morphology at our finger-tips; henceforward we can concentrate more particularly on Syntax and Analysis (*i.e.*, the logical construction of speech) and the history of Language (*i.e.*, how we came to arrange our speech as we do in order to convey our thoughts).

Our Reading will proceed from narrative and lyric to essays, argument and criticism, and the pupil will learn to try his own hand at writing this kind of thing. Many lessons—on whatever subject—will take the form of debates; and the place of individual or choral recitation will be taken by dramatic performances, with special attention to plays in which an argument is stated in dramatic form.

Mathematics—Algebra, Geometry, and the more advanced kind of Arithmetic—will now enter into the syllabus and take its place as what it really is: not a separate "subject" but a sub-department of Logic. It is neither more nor less than the rule of the syllogism in its particular application to number and measurement, and should be taught as such, instead of being, for some, a dark mystery, and for others, a special revelation, neither illuminating nor illuminated by any other part of knowledge.

History, aided by a simple system of ethics derived from the Grammar of Theology, will provide much suitable material for discussion: Was the behaviour of this statesman justified? What was the effect of such an enactment? What are the arguments for and against this or that form of government? We shall thus get an introduction to Constitutional History—a subject meaningless to the young child, but of absorbing interest to those who are prepared to argue and debate. *Theology* itself will furnish material for argument about conduct and morals; and should have its scope extended by a simplified course of dogmatic theology (*i.e.*, the rational structure of Christian thought), clarifying the relations between the dogma and the ethics, and lending itself to that application of ethical principles in particular instances which is properly called casuistry. *Geography* and the *Sciences* will all likewise provide material for Dialectic.

But above all, we must not neglect the material which is so abundant in the pupils' own daily life. There is a delightful passage in Leslie Paul's *The Living Hedge* which tells how a number of small boys enjoyed themselves for days arguing about an extraordinary shower of rain which had fallen in their town—a shower so localised that it left one half of the main street wet and the other dry. Could one, they argued, properly say that it had rained that day *on* or *over* the town or only *in* the town? How many drops of water were required to constitute rain? and so on. Argument about this led on to a host of similar problems about rest and motion, sleep and waking, *est* and *non est*, and the infinitesimal division of time. The whole passage is an admirable example of the spontaneous development of the ratiocinative faculty and the natural and proper thirst of the awakening reason for definition of terms and exactness of statement. All events are food for such an appetite. An umpire's decision; the degree to which one may transgress the spirit of a regulation without being trapped by the letter; on such questions as these, children are born casuists, and their natural propensity only needs to be developed and trained—and, especially, brought into an intelligible relationship with events in the grown-up world. The newspapers are full of good material for such exercises: legal decisions, on the one hand, in cases where the cause at issue is not too abstruse; on the other, fallacious reasoning and muddle-headed argument, with which the correspondence columns of certain papers one could name are abundantly stocked.

Wherever the matter for Dialectic is found, it is, of course, highly important that attention should be focused

upon the beauty and economy of a fine demonstration or
a well-turned argument, lest veneration should wholly
die. Criticism must not be merely destructive; though
at the same time both teacher and pupils must be ready
to detect fallacy, slipshod reasoning, ambiguity, irrele-
vance and redundancy, and to pounce upon them
like rats.

This is the moment when precis-writing may be usefully undertaken; together with such exercises as the
writing of an essay, and the reduction of it, when
written, by 25 or 50 per cent.

It will, doubtless, be objected that to encourage young
persons at the Pert Age to browbeat, correct and argue
with their elders will render them perfectly intolerable.
My answer is that children of that age are intolerable
anyhow; and that their natural argumentativeness may
just as well be canalised to good purpose as allowed to
run away into the sands. It may, indeed, be rather less
obtrusive at home if it is disciplined in school; and,
anyhow, elders who have abandoned the wholesome
principle that children should be seen and not heard
have no one to blame but themselves. The teachers, to be
sure, will have to mind their step, or they may get more
than they bargained for. All children sit in judgment on
their masters; and if the Chaplain's sermon or the
Headmistress's annual Speech-day address should by any
chance afford an opening for the point of the critical
wedge, that wedge will go home the more forcibly under
the weight of the Dialectical hammer, wielded by a
practised hand. That is why I said that the teachers
themselves would need to undergo the discipline of the
Trivium before they set out to impose it on their charges.

Once again: the contents of the syllabus at this stage
may be anything you like. The "subjects" supply material; but they are all to be regarded as mere grist for the
mental mill to work upon. The pupils should be encour-

aged to go and forage for their own information, and so guided towards the proper use of libraries and books of reference, and shown how to tell which sources are authoritative and which are not.

Towards the close of this stage, the pupils will probably be beginning to discover for themselves that their knowledge and experience are insufficient, and that their trained intelligences need a great deal more material to chew upon. The imagination—usually dormant during the Pert age—will re-awaken, and prompt them to suspect the limitations of logic and reason. This means that they are passing into the Poetic age and are ready to embark on the study of Rhetoric. The doors of the storehouse of knowledge should now be thrown open for them to browse about as they will. The things once learned by rote will be seen in new contexts; the things once coldly analysed can now be brought together to form a new synthesis; here and there a sudden insight will bring about that most exciting of all discoveries: the realisation that a truism is true.

It is difficult to map out any general syllabus for the study of Rhetoric: a certain freedom is demanded. In literature, appreciation should be again allowed to take the lead over destructive criticism; and self-expression in writing can go forward, with its tools now sharpened to cut clean and observe proportion. Any child that already shows a disposition to specialise should be given his head: for, when the use of the tools has been well and truly learned it is available for any study whatever. It would be well, I think, that each pupil should learn to do one, or two, subjects really well, while taking a few classes in subsidiary subjects so as to keep his mind open to the inter-relations of all knowledge. Indeed, at this stage, our difficulty will be to keep "subjects" apart; for as Dialectic will have shown all branches of learning to be inter-related, so Rhetoric will tend to show that all knowledge is one. To show this, and show why it is so, is pre-eminently the task of the Mistress-science. But whether Theology is studied or not, we should at least insist that children who seem inclined to specialise on the mathematical and scientific side should be obliged to attend some lessons in the Humanities and *vice versa*. At this stage also, the Latin Grammar, having done its work, may be dropped for those who prefer to carry on their language studies on the modern side; while those who are likely never to have any great use or aptitude for mathematics might also be allowed to rest, more or less, upon their oars. Generally speaking: whatsoever is *mere* apparatus may now be allowed to fall into the background, while the trained mind is gradually prepared for specialisation in the "subjects" which, when the Trivium is completed, it should be perfectly well equipped to tackle on its own. The final synthesis of the Trivium—the presentation and public defence of the thesis—should be restored in some form; perhaps as a kind of "leaving examination" during the last term at school.

The scope of Rhetoric depends also on whether the pupil is to be turned out into the world at the age of 16 or whether he is to proceed to public school and/or university. Since, really, Rhetoric should be taken at about 14, the first category of pupil should study Grammar from about 9 to 11, and Dialectic from 12 to 14; his last two school years would then be devoted to Rhetoric, which, in his case, would be of a fairly specialised and vocational kind, suiting him to enter immediately upon some practical career. A pupil of the second category would finish the Dialectical course in his Preparatory School, and take Rhetoric during his first two years at his Public School. At 16, he would be ready to start upon those "subjects" which are proposed for his later study at the university: and this part of his education will correspond to the mediaeval Quadrivium. What this amounts to is that the ordinary pupil, whose formal education ends at 16, will take the Trivium only; whereas scholars will take both Trivium and Quadrivium.

Is the Trivium, then, a sufficient education for life? Properly taught, I believe that it should be. At the end of the Dialectic, the children will probably seem to be far behind their coaevals brought up on old-fashioned "modern" methods, so far as detailed knowledge of specific subjects is concerned. But after the age of 14 they should be able to overhaul the others hand over fist. Indeed, I am not at all sure that a pupil thoroughly proficient in the Trivium would not be fit to proceed immediately to the university at the age of 16, thus proving himself the equal of his mediaeval counterpart, whose precocity astonished us at the beginning of this discussion. This, to be sure, would make hay of the public-school system, and disconcert the universities very much—it would, for example, make quite a different thing of the Oxford and Cambridge Boat-race. But I am not here to consider the feelings of academic bodies; I am concerned only with the proper training of the mind to encounter and deal with the formidable mass of undigested problems presented to it by the modern world. For the tools of learning are the same, in any and every subject; and the person who knows how to use them will, at any age, get the mastery of a new subject in half the time and with a quarter of the effort expended by the person who has not the tools at his command. To learn six subjects without remembering how they were learnt does nothing to ease the approach to a seventh; to have learnt and remembered the art of learning makes the approach to every subject an open door.

It is clear that the successful teaching of this neo-mediaeval curriculum will depend even more than usual upon the working together of the whole teaching staff towards a common purpose. Since no subject is considered as an end in itself, any kind of rivalry in the staff-room will be sadly out of place. The fact that a pupil is, unfortunately, obliged, for some reason, to miss the History period on Fridays, or the Shakespeare class on Tuesdays, or even to omit a whole subject in favour of some other subject, must not be allowed to cause any heart-burnings—the essential is that he should acquire the method of learning in whatever medium suits him best. If human nature suffers under this blow to one's professional pride in one's own subject, there is comfort in the thought that the end-of-term examination results will not be affected; for the papers will be so arranged as to be an examination in method, by whatever means.

I will add that it is highly important that every teacher should, for his or her own sake, be qualified and required to teach in all three parts of the Trivium; otherwise the Masters of Dialectic, especially, might find their minds hardening into a permanent adolescence. For this reason, teachers in Preparatory Schools should also take Rhetoric classes in the Public Schools to which they are attached; or, if they are not so attached, then by arrangement in other schools in the same neighbourhood. Alternatively, a few preliminary classes in Rhetoric might be taken in Preparatory Schools from the age of 13 onwards.

Before concluding these necessarily very sketchy suggestions, I ought to say why I think it necessary, in these days, to go back to a discipline which we had discarded. The truth is that for the last 300 years or so we have been living upon our educational capital. The post-Renaissance world, bewildered and excited by the profusion of new "subjects" offered to it, broke away from the old discipline (which had, indeed, become sadly dull and

stereotyped in its practical application) and imagined
that henceforward it could, as it were, disport itself
happily in its new and extended Quadrivium without
passing through the Trivium. But the scholastic tradition, though broken and maimed, still lingered in the
public schools and universities: Milton, however much
he protested against it, was formed by it—the debate of
the Fallen Angels, and the disputation of Abdiel with
Satan have the tool-marks of the Schools upon them, and
might, incidentally, profitably figure as set passages for
our Dialectical studies. Right down to the 19th century,
our public affairs were mostly managed, and our books
and journals were for the most part written, by people
brought up in homes, and trained in places, where that
tradition was still alive in the memory and almost in the
blood. Just so, many people to-day who are atheist or
agnostic in religion, are governed in their conduct by a
code of Christian ethics which is so rooted in their unconscious assumptions that it never occurs to them to
question it. But one cannot live on capital for ever. A
tradition, however firmly rooted, if it is never watered,
though it dies hard, yet in the end it dies. And to-day a
great number—perhaps the majority—of the men and
women who handle our affairs, write our books and our
newspapers, carry out research, present our plays and our
films, speak from our platforms and pulpits—yes, and
who educate our young people, have never, even in a
lingering traditional memory, undergone the scholastic
discipline. Less and less do the children who come to be
educated bring any of that tradition with them. We have
lost the tools of learning—the axe and the wedge, the
hammer and the saw, the chisel and the plane—that
were so adaptable to all tasks. Instead of them, we have
merely a set of complicated jigs, each of which will do
but one task and no more, and in using which eye and
hand receive no training, so that no man ever sees the

work as a whole or "looks to the end of the work." What
use is it to pile task on task and prolong the days of
labour, if at the close the chief object is left unattained?
It is not the fault of the teachers—they work only too
hard already. The combined folly of a civilisation that
has forgotten its own roots is forcing them to shore up
the tottering weight of an educational structure that is
built upon sand. They are doing for their pupils the
work which the pupils themselves ought to do. For the
sole true end of education is simply this: to teach men
how to learn for themselves; and whatever instruction
fails to do this is effort spent in vain.

LTL 1-30

Poetry

FOR TIMOTHY, IN THE COINHERENCE

"Tutti tirati sono, e tutti tirano" —
(*Paradiso* xxviii. 129)

Consider, O Lord, Timothy, Thy servants' servant.
  (We give him this title, as to Thy servant the Pope,
  Not knowing a better. Him too Thy ministers were
    observant
To vest in white and adorn with a silk cope.)

Thy servant lived with Thy servants in the exchange
  Of affection; he condescended to them from the
    dignity
  Of an innocent mind; they bent to him with benignity
From the rarefied Alps of their intellectual range.

Hierarchy flourished, with no resentment
  For the unsheathed claw or the hand raised in
    correction;
  Small wild charities took root beneath the Protection,
Garden-escapes from the Eden of our contentment.

Daily we came short in the harder human relation,
  Only in this easier obeying, Lord, Thy commands;
  Meekly we washed his feet, meekly he licked our
    hands —
Beseech Thee, overlook not this mutual grace of
    salvation.

Canst Thou accept our pitiful good behaving,
  Stooping to share at our hand that best we keep for
    the beast?
  Sir, receive the alms, though least, and bestowed on
    the least,
Save us, and save somehow with us the means of our
    saving.

138

Dante in the Eighth Heaven beheld love's law
   Run up and down on the infinite golden stairway;
   Angels, men, brutes, plants, matter, up that fairway
All by love's cords are drawn, said he, and draw.

Thou that before the Fall didst make pre-emption
   Of Adam, restore the privilege of the Garden,
   Where he to the beasts was namer, tamer, and
      warden;
Buy back his household and all in the world's
      redemption.

When the Ark of the new life grounds upon Ararat
   Grant us to carry into the rainbow's light,
   In a basket of gratitude, the small, milk-white
Silken identity of Timothy, our cat.

O holy God, Holy and strong, Holy and Immortal, have mercy upon us. By the wood and the iron, by the wormwood and the gall, by the water and the blood, have mercy upon us.

EC 183